SILVER SPOON KIDS

SILVER SPOON KIDS

HOW SUCCESSFUL PARENTS RAISE
RESPONSIBLE CHILDREN

EILEEN GALLO, PH.D.,
AND JON GALLO, J.D.

Contemporary Books

Chicago   New York   San Francisco   Lisbon   London   Madrid   Mexico City
Milan   New Delhi   San Juan   Seoul   Singapore   Sydney   Toronto

Library of Congress Cataloging-in-Publication Data

Gallo, Eileen F.
    Silver spoon kids : How successful parents raise responsible children /
Eileen F. Gallo, Jon J. Gallo.
        p.   cm.
    Includes index.
    ISBN 0-8092-9437-0
    1. Child rearing—United States.   2. Responsibility in children.
3. Wealth—United States.   I. Gallo, Jon J.   II. Title.

HQ769.G249   2001
649'.1'0973—dc21   2001037286

Contemporary Books

A Division of The McGraw-Hill Companies

2 3 4 5 6 7 8 9 0   DOC/DOC   0 9 8 7 6 5 4 3 2

ISBN 0-8092-9437-0

This book was set in Bembo
Printed and bound by Quebecor Martinsburg

Cover and interior design by Nick Panos
Cover photographs copyright © Image Club Graphics

McGraw-Hill books are available at special quantity discounts to use as premiums
and sales promotions, or for use in corporate training programs. For more
information, please write to the Director of Special Sales, Professional Publishing,
McGraw-Hill, Two Penn Plaza, New York, NY 10121-2298. Or contact your local
bookstore.

This book is printed on acid-free paper.

To our children, Valerie, Donald, and Kevin,
and our granddaughter, Emily

Contents

Foreword ix

Acknowledgments xi

Introduction xiii

1 Affluence Is a Double-Edged Sword 1

2 Keeping Your Child's Development on Track 17

3 Money Personalities 37

4 The Value of Values 59

5 Talking with Your Kids About Money 85

6 Allowances: Giving Your Child More than Money 117

7 Diversity: How to "Unshelter" Your Child 133

8 Give and You Shall Receive 153

9 Family Wealth Planning 177

10 Parenting in an Age of Change: Dealing with New or Unusual Money Situations 203

11 Invest in Your Child's Future 231

Appendix 241

Bibliography 249

Index 257

Foreword

by Kevin J. Gallo, an adult child

It's a unique experience being the offspring of parents writing a book for other parents about raising children in an age of affluence. When my parents began this journey, I didn't know how to describe the book they were writing. Friends would ask, and I would just say, "They're writing a book about how not to give money to your kids." Through their writing process, I have learned what this book is actually about. It's about setting a good example for your kids, which they have done (for the most part). It's about demystifying money, which I learned early on in my childhood. If I had money, I spent it. If I was broke, I didn't. No mystery there. It's also about human development . . . not the sex education class we had in high school, but a close reading of the *Homo sapiens* psyche . . . a study of how people react to money and why they react the way they do.

This book has seen more drafts than an air-conditioning repairman. Even the title was the subject of debate. We had an interesting discussion about it during a family dinner that included my parents, my stepsiblings, their spouses, and myself. I admit I was hesitant to participate in the conversation, but then I remembered that my parents paid for me to attend Loyola Marymount University to earn a bachelor's degree in English with an emphasis on writing. Suddenly, I felt compelled to assist them in any way I could. I submitted several suggestions for review. I thought *Who Wants to Raise a Millionaire?* captured the essence of their book while appealing to the current pop culture fad. *I Never Promised You a Rolls* was another suggestion, combining the book's theme with a popular colloquialism. Admittedly, *When Money Does Grow on Trees: Providing a Ladder for Your Lass or Laddie* was a bit too Scottish. So, with the help of an unabridged dictionary, I plunged into the depths of the English language, searching for meaning and consonance. The result, *The Confluence of Affluence and Influence*, unfortunately fell short of my parents' dream book title.

Then, on their own, they came up with *Silver Spoon Kids*, the title you see today. They polled several members of our family, as well as friends and business associates, and everyone agreed that it sounded pretty good. When I asked them if they would have a problem with their book bearing a title similar to a popular television series starring Ricky Schroder, they asked in unison, "Who's Ricky Schroder?" The search for a title was over.

This book will work for you and your family. It's already worked for my family. Instead of haranguing our parents for cash, my stepsiblings and I have learned how much more rewarding it is for us to face our financial issues on our own.

The gratification we have felt from balancing our own budgets, saving up for big purchases, and making financially sound decisions supersedes any emergency loan, gift, or "helping out" we could have received from our parents. In fact, we found a way to show our appreciation for what we learned and contribute to our parents' foray into literature. The first draft of this book was printed on paper recycled from all of the credit card offers we have joyfully discarded over the years!

Acknowledgments

We are indebted to many people who have contributed in many different ways to make *Silver Spoon Kids* possible:

Zo Byrnes, Jilliene Schenkel, Judy Barber, John Levy, and Peter Karoff for their invaluable assistance and for unselfishly sharing their concepts and concerns.

Stuart Ende, Sherry Brent, Wendy Darby, and Sharon Dunas for their encouragement.

Art and Patty Antin, Ken and Katrina Carlson, Al Wroblewski, Elinor Livingston, Mary Micucci, Jane Downs, Arnold Kahn, Barbara Wilson, Marlo and Greg Longstreet, Sarah Pillsbury, Heidi Frey Greenwald, Helen and Jim Zukin, Nina Sabban, Janet Bodner, Arthur and Arlene Schwimmer, Bonny Dore, Stephan Poulter, Jerry Florence, Pat Byrnes, Brent Kessell, Andy Goldfarb, Julie Flapan, David Lehrer, Roger Hastings, Audrey Cahn, Christina Pickles, Ann Reynolds, Julie and Richard Kagan, Christie William, Jean Brincko, J. Brin and Barbara Shulman, and Joyce Bivans, who shared anecdotes, experiences, and ideas.

Bruce Wexler, who forced us to focus; our agent, Caroline Carney, who was a continual source of support and encouragement; and our editor at Contemporary Books, Judith McCarthy, who read every word, found every inconsistency, and offered invaluable suggestions for improvement.

Introduction

Are you confused about how and when to talk to your child about money issues?

Are you worried that your child will grow up with a sense of entitlement and never take responsibility for helping those who have less?

Are you upset about the overly materialistic messages with which the media is bombarding your son or daughter?

Do you live in an upscale community where you're concerned about the values of some of the adults and children?

Do you wonder how you can help your child become a responsible money manager when his friends have credit cards with no limits and their parents buy them everything they want?

Is your greatest concern as a parent that your comfortable lifestyle will somehow "corrupt" your child, turning him into a substance-abusing, unmotivated adolescent or young adult?

We ask these questions because they weigh heavily on the minds of many parents these days, and not just parents who are multimillionaires. Raising a child in an age of affluence is an issue that confronts parents with a wide range of incomes. Solidly middle-class families are struggling with many of the same situations that upper-income families are grappling with. The influence of affluence is pervasive. It's not just that more people have more money than ever before. In some instances, children grow up unmotivated because they know they will inherit a significant sum on their twenty-first birthday. In other instances, the problem is psychological—some parents don't spend the time necessary establishing the relationships and instilling the values that counteract negative societal messages about money.

In other words, you don't have to be superrich to benefit from this book (although it doesn't hurt if you are). If you simply live in a nice community and make a good living, you're likely to find *Silver Spoon Kids* relevant to your child raising. As someone once said, you don't have to be a Rockefeller to raise a spoiled kid.

Not that the point of this book is how to avoid raising spoiled kids. Although that is one worthy goal, it is only one of many. The impact of affluence on children is multifaceted, and it can result in a wide variety of effects. A loss of ambition, an inability to handle money responsibly, feelings of guilt, a fear of failure, an unearned sense of privilege and accomplishment—these are just some of the potential negative impacts.

We don't believe, however, that affluence is bad. We'll say it here for the first time but not for the last: having money is a good thing if you are a parent. One of our objectives in writing this book is to help you capitalize on affluence as a child-raising tool rather than let it become a problem. Well-to-do families can provide incredible opportunities for their children, opportunities that will not only foster emotionally healthy kids, but enable them to become responsible managers of money. Before discussing how the book will help you take advantage of these opportunities, we'd like to share the story of how this book came to be written. Its origins will give you a sense of why we feel strongly about this topic, not only as authors, but as parents ourselves.

Becoming Aware of How People Handle Money

A book review in the Sunday *New York Times* changed the course of our lives. It was 1986. We had gotten married the year before and between us had three kids; we were "remarried with children." Eileen was working on her doctorate in psychology, and Jon was a partner in a Los Angeles law firm, where he specialized in estate planning.

That Sunday the *Times* reviewed Susan Littwin's *The Postponed Generation: Why American Youth Are Growing Up Later*. Littwin proposed that an entire generation of young people were in the process of postponing the responsibilities and autonomy of adulthood. As parents and counselors, we had started to deal with some of the issues Littwin wrote about, as had many of our friends and clients, but the review of Littwin's book catalyzed our first collaborative effort: an article published by the UCLA Estate Planning Institute titled "Estate Planning for the Postponed Generation." Other articles combining psychology and estate planning soon followed.

When Eileen settled on a topic for her doctoral dissertation, she chose to examine the emotional issues involved in sudden wealth. The talk shows and Sunday supplements were featuring stories of people who had won the lottery or unexpectedly inherited large sums of money and were devastated by the experience. Eileen undertook a two-year study of the emotional factors associated with sudden wealth in an attempt to find out why some people adapted well and others did not.

As part of the process, interviewees were asked about their childhood experiences with money and the early money messages they received from their parents. As the interviews continued, a fascinating pattern began to emerge. Interviewees were answering questions that Eileen wasn't asking! In particular, they were concerned about the effect of their money on their children. Eileen wanted to know about their childhood; the interviewees wanted to talk about their children. Several posed a variation of the same question: "How much money does it take to ruin a child?"

In the evenings, we would discuss the fact that we had a number of affluent friends and clients who were raising responsible, well-mannered, and motivated kids. Pretty soon the answers to the question Eileen wasn't asking turned into a question for us: just what was it that some parents knew that others didn't—what was it that they were doing right?

It took us about three years of research, interviews, client work, and reading to determine that the answer to raising responsible, emotionally healthy children is a combination of factors: the need to demystify money, an understanding of fundamental psychological principles of human development, a clear concept of your values, your relationship with money, and the money messages that you are modeling for your children.

That research also led to *Silver Spoon Kids*. For more than thirty years, Jon has lectured nationally to financial professionals on taxes and estate-planning topics. After Eileen finished her doctoral dissertation, we began teaching together, combining psychological insights into the effects of affluence with technical discussions of taxes and estate planning. As a psychotherapist specializing in the emotional issues of wealth and an attorney who helps the affluent transfer family wealth to younger generations and charities, we were able to bring a unique perspective to these issues. Our joint presentations soon led to our being asked by New York University to help create the NYU Family Wealth Institute. We're members of the advisory board and regular speakers at the institute, which meets in Manhattan during the first week of May each year. As requests for our presentations multiplied, we formed the Gallo Institute as the educational arm of our separate practices. Through the Gallo Institute, we have spoken to many leading financial professionals and their clients. A few years ago, we added a new seminar focusing on children, money, and values. It quickly became one of the Gallo Institute's most popular offerings and led to our decision to write this book. For more information about the Gallo Institute and our presentations, visit www.galloinsti tute.org.

We wrote this book with a specific agenda in mind. First, we wanted to be sure it would be useful for parents no matter what age their children might be. Whether you have a newborn baby, a toddler, an adolescent, or a young adult, you will find concepts and suggestions that apply to your child. Second, we did not want to write an anti-money book. We do not believe that money is the root of all evil or that an abundance of it does irreparable harm to kids. The problem is money unaccompanied by values. As a result, we emphasize the importance of communicating your values to your kids, especially regarding your "money behaviors." Third, we were intent on writing a practical book rather than an academic or theoretical one. This is a book that's designed to be used. That's why you'll find answers to some of the most common questions parents struggle with. For instance, what is the "right" answer when your six-year-old asks you how much money you have? How should you respond when your twelve-year-old asks for an increase in her allowance? What about your sixteen-year-old high school sophomore who wants a credit card because "everyone else has one"? Or what action should you take when your twenty-two-year-old, who has maxed out her credit cards, wants to move back home to save rent money? Fourth, we hope to provide you with an understanding of your relationship with money so that you can help your children establish a money relationship untainted by whatever negative tendencies you might have.

Ultimately, what we want you to take away from this book are the knowledge and tools to help your child live a happy and meaningful life—a life that is facilitated rather than hurt by her money relationships.

From Money Meanings to Money Talk

Throughout *Silver Spoon Kids*, you'll find a mix of practical advice, stories, and explanations of the "why" behind the issues we address. As important as it is for you to know what to do to raise good kids in affluent environments, it's just as important for you to understand why you should do it. You're much more likely to do the right thing if you have a good reason for doing it.

To that end, we'll explain the psychological meaning of money and how people form different money relationships (i.e., being a spender versus being a miser) and how these relationships impact their children. We'll also look at child developmental stages and how affluence can cause problems during these stages. In addition, we'll focus on the importance of defining and articulating values and how these actions can serve as a strong defense against the negative aspects of affluence.

Just about every chapter will contain usable material, from checklists to self-tests. You'll find ideas that will help you translate the money messages you're sending your children as well as advice on how to change those messages (if you're not satisfied with what you're communicating). Techniques for fostering a philanthropic interest in your child, for answering the most common money questions kids ask, and for dealing with the tricky subject of allowances are just a few examples of the practical advice you'll encounter. In addition, each chapter contains "Silver Nuggets"— boxed, one- or two-sentence bits of wisdom and advice that you can quickly put to use and activities for you and your children to do together.

Finally, we have many great stories to tell. We've drawn these stories from our experiences with our clients as well as from ones told to us by friends, associates, and attendees at our workshops. We'll also share anecdotes that relate to our own experiences as parents. These various stories range from humorous to touching, but all have a lesson to impart. There are stories that illustrate all the mistakes affluent parents can make, and there are motivational ones that demonstrate model parenting behaviors. In all of the stories, we have changed the names of the participants, and many of the stories are composites drawn from our joint experiences.

A Book We Wish We Had Read When We Were Just Starting Out

Parenting can be a challenge whether you're rich or poor. In fact, it's probably much more difficult to be a parent if you're working two jobs to pay the rent and feed the kids, living in crowded quarters, and worrying about crime and drugs in the neighborhood. On the other hand, it's a mistake to believe that affluence can make parenting easy. If you have a decent amount of money and are living in relative comfort, it's easy to be lulled into a false sense of security. Just because you live in a neighborhood with good schools and can afford to buy your child nice things doesn't mean that you're home free. In reality, your child faces psychological and money issues that you need to be aware of and act upon.

Some pundits have suggested that no adult should be allowed to become a parent until she or he passes a test to qualify for the job. Behind that facetious idea, however, is a valid concept that applies to this book: people have not been educated to parent in an affluent society. Part of the problem is that many couples are first-generation affluents. They grew up in households where money was scarce. As a result, they lack adequate models for their parenting attitudes and actions. Their parents may have been wonderful, loving moms and dads, but they faced a different set of challenges. They may have learned valuable lessons from their parents, but there are different lessons that need to be taught.

The other part of the problem, however, applies whether your parents were rich or poor. Society has changed. The combination of family values and religious beliefs that used to influence kids as they were growing up has been diluted. In its place is unprecedented affluence, and many individuals in our society have no compunction about "showing off." Or, in the immortal words of the Nathan Lane character in *The Producers*, "If you've got it, flaunt it." A generation ago, it was rare for people to tear down attractive three-bedroom houses and replace them with homes twice as large. Back then, few parents bought their kids luxury cars for their sixteenth birthdays or took them on vacations to three different continents before they were ten years old. Years ago, commercials, television shows, and movies were not as slickly effective in pushing excessive consumerism, and there was no such thing as a twenty-five-year-old dot-com billionaire.

What all this boils down to is this: being an affluent parent comes with responsibilities. It's not just the responsibility of preventing money from harming your child, but the responsibility of using that money to parent in positive ways.

We wish we had learned the lessons of *Silver Spoon Kids* when our kids were younger. It would have helped us avoid a number of mistakes. We hope that you will benefit from our mistakes, our research, and our ideas and become the best parent you can be.

Affluence Is a Double-Edged Sword

The past decade has been one of the most affluent in history. Thus, we should have more resources than ever before to raise happy, emotionally healthy children. Affluence, however, is a double-edged sword. For instance, affluence

- allows us to raise our children in comfort but also allows us to overindulge them
- gives us the ability to buy products and services that help our kids learn and develop but also makes it easier to focus on materialism
- increases the choices available to our sons and daughters but also overloads them with activities and pressures them to succeed
- enables them to be involved in philanthropy but also creates children with a sense of entitlement

Although affluence has always been a double-edged sword, it has become an increasingly sharp and dangerous one in recent years. We'd like to give you a sense of some of the factors and trends that have made it increasingly difficult for affluent parents to raise emotionally healthy children. First, though, please look at the box, "The Effects of Affluence." It provides a quick overview of the potential positive and negative effects of affluence.

You Don't Have to Be Rich to Be Affluent

Once upon a time, affluence was restricted to the upper class. It's only relatively recently—the last twenty years or so—that the definition has broadened. In the late '90s and into the twenty-first century, however, we've seen affluence become a middle-class phenomenon. The accumulated monies in retirement plans (passed down from one generation to the next) and widespread participation in the stock market have enabled more people to live an affluent lifestyle. Dow Jones & Company introduced the industrial index in 1897, and on its first day the market closed at 40.94. It took another seventy-six years for the Dow Jones Industrial index to close above 1,000 (in 1972). By 1995 it went above 5,000 for the first time. It took only four more years before it broke the 10,000 barrier.

Another important factor is that the parents of baby boomers are passing on large sums of money to their adult children. Experts estimate that more than $50 trillion will pass through the inheritance system in the next twenty years. On top of that, the increase in dual-income households is making it possible for families to afford homes, cars, and travel that were denied to single-income households in years past. Speaking of jobs, we're not only seeing more people making more money than ever before, but we're seeing them make it at younger ages. This trend has been fueled by the proliferation of high-tech companies—companies frequently run by people in their twenties and thirties. Even when the dot-com wave came crashing back to Earth, it left many young dot-

THE EFFECTS OF AFFLUENCE

Positive	Negative
Financial security	Lack of motivation to work/achieve
Freedom to learn/ explore	Laziness
More interesting things to do	Activity overload
Exposure to the finer things in life	Overindulgence
Philanthropic opportunities	Sense of entitlement
Friendships with other bright, affluent kids	Insularity and snobbery
Appreciation for the rewards of hard work and ambition	Extreme materialism

com millionaires in its wake. Just as significantly, the growing use of credit cards, the increase in credit card limits, and the ease in obtaining loans based on home equity all have contributed to the trend of "virtual affluence."

It's not difficult to make a case that our purchasing power is greater than ever before. *Purchasing power*, however, isn't synonymous with *affluence*. Let's define our terms. Or rather, let's start out with what affluence is not. First, it is not exclusively defined by your net worth, where you live, or what your profession is. Certainly doctors and lawyers who make six-figure incomes and live in exclusive suburbs are affluent, but many middle-class families also qualify as affluent. Let's say two parents both work as teachers, and each receives a rather modest $45,000 salary. Yet their combined salaries, a small inheritance the woman received when her parents died, and the use of credit allows them to take vacations to the south of France each summer, have a swimming pool, and send their two children to one of the country's best tennis camps. Although they may live in a middle-of-the-road suburb, their children are certainly exposed to activities that connote wealth, and they also associate with children and families who have a significant amount of money.

At the opposite end of the spectrum, there's Hetty Green. We don't consider her affluent even though she inherited more than $7 million when she was twenty-one, and when she died sixty-one years later, she was one of the wealthiest women in America. We'll come back to Green later.

To a certain extent, affluence, like beauty, is in the eye of the beholder. Although it is absurd to think that someone on welfare might consider himself affluent, it is not at all absurd to extend the traditional definition beyond the wealthiest members of society.

Are you affluent? The easy answer is yes, because you probably would not have picked up this book unless you were concerned about how your lifestyle or the wealth found in your community is impacting your child. But we don't recommend getting hung up on the semantics of the term. Instead, look over the following list, and place a check mark next to any of the items that apply to you (and your family):

SILVER NUGGET

Think of five individuals or couples whom you consider your closest friends. You can also include siblings. Do you consider them affluent or nonaffluent? What criteria did you use to make these judgments?

☐ We usually have money left over for luxuries.

☐ Our child has friends who have considerably more money than we do.

☐ We regularly take nice vacations.

☐ There are times when we feel as if we're giving our child more (in terms of presents, lessons, camps, etc.) than we should.

☐ We live in a community or area of the city that is considered prestigious or at least contains a significant number of upper-middle-class residents.

☐ We make liberal use of credit to maintain our lifestyle.

☐ In the next few years, we expect our net worth to increase significantly (because of job promotions, investments, inheritance).

☐ When it comes to food, clothing, furniture, consumer electronics, and education, we believe in buying the best in at least one of these areas.

☐ We are a dual-income household.

☐ We employ nannies or au pairs, a lawn care service, maid, stockbroker, lawyer, and accountant (place a check mark if you employ two or more).

☐ We plan on moving to a home or condominium or already own one.

If you've checked two or more of these items, affluence will probably impact your kids. The question is, will it be a positive or negative impact?

Troubling Trends

For some people, the American dream of affluence has turned into the nightmare of raising a generation of spoiled children who are growing up to become self-centered, self-indulgent adults. What has turned the dream into a nightmare? Let's look at some of the more significant trends.

• **Extreme materialism.** Highly sophisticated advertising—much of it targeting teens and preteens—urges them to buy and suggests that they're entitled to whatever the product is, no matter how much it costs. The commingled message is something like this: *You deserve a break today, so go buy X, Y, or Z and it will make you handsome, sexy, happy, and cool.* The emphasis on brand names coupled with a cynical, self-indulgent tone can be found in countless commercials. Although materialistic messages have been around for a long time, they used to be accompanied by a strong social value system. Parents, church, and school instilled values such as honesty, charity, and responsibility, and the media reinforced these values. Today, these values aren't as strong, and as a result, materialism has much more power over children. When kids don't believe in the importance of charity or the concept of living a responsible life, they are much more vulnerable to the negative impact of affluence. They are much more likely to become selfish and spoiled because the "balancing" underlying values are weaker than in the past.

• **Impermanence.** Nothing lasts very long, and we are losing the comfort that comes from dealing with the familiar. More than

SILVER NUGGET

Ask your child to name his favorite commercial and recite its jingle or slogan. Is this jingle or slogan conveying the values you want to instill in your child? Or does it seem to be pushing conspicuous consumption, elitism, snobbery, or unethical behavior?

---

two-thirds of all consumer goods available for purchase today did not exist thirty years ago. In just about every city, long-standing buildings and even entire neighborhoods are being demolished to make way for "new and improved" versions. Even in the suburbs, "teardowns" of perfectly fine homes ravage old neighborhoods, and bigger, new homes are erected in their place. We see this impermanence in computer technology, where hardware and software are outdated almost from the moment they are installed. Jobs, too, no longer last a lifetime. In fact, because of downsizing, mergers, and other trends, people move from job to job with alarming speed.

This impermanence can breed cynicism and greed. "Get it while you can" is a catchphrase of adolescents and young adults. Without the bulwarks of tradition and stability, these adolescents and young adults are much more likely to develop unhealthy attitudes toward money-related matters. Wealth, like everything else in society, seems fleeting. Therefore, why not spend it fast before it's all gone? This impermanence also robs many young people of ambition; why try to make a lot of money or work hard at a job when everything is so evanescent?

• **Lack of time.** One of the most telling symbols of our era is the use of Palm Pilots to schedule children's activities. In many affluent homes, kids have tightly packed schedules that include everything from private lessons to camps to therapy sessions to sports, and parents need computerized devices to keep track of everything they're involved in. In a scary way, the kids' schedules mirror the schedules of their parents (especially if both parents are working). Little time exists for families to eat meals together, to play board games, to sit around and talk after dinner, to go for walks, or to do all of the things that used to be part of the family gestalt. David Elkind, author of *The Hurried Child: Growing Up Too Fast Too Soon*, observes that hurried children are being forced to take on the trappings of adulthood before they are prepared to deal with them. Passing on values and beliefs from parent to child, therefore, is difficult to do because they aren't passed on at one sitting; they require repeated interactions over many years, and some families don't have time for this repetition. Kids develop their own values, and in affluent households, these values often are focused on things rather than on more meaningful ideas.

• **Electronic media.** Newton Minow, the former Federal Communications Commission (FCC) chairman who described television as "a vast wasteland," said in 1989 that most Americans by the age of eighteen will have spent far more time in front of the television than they will have spent in school. Although not all television is bad, much of what kids watch—especially the commercials—pushes them to want "more and better." Television shows that offer viewers the chance to be millionaires place an undue emphasis on becoming instantly wealthy. When kids aren't watching television, they're often online. Again, the problem isn't the medium itself—computers, like television, can be a good learning tool—as much as what it prevents kids from doing. Engaging in real conversations with real people—parents, teachers, coaches, friends—is how kids mature emotionally and become socialized. Edward M. Hallowell, M.D., of Harvard Medical School, goes so far as to say that face-to-face communication is the key to what counts in life, from a happy family to physical health and longevity. Participating in activities with friends and adults provides experiences that help shape values. When kids are watching a TV screen or computer monitor or playing video games for hours each day, they are robbed of these conversations and activities. It's no wonder that many of them are emotionally stunted and do not develop the solid values that keep them from becoming spoiled, entitled, snobbish, or unmotivated.

All these trends and developments affect the way we raise children today versus how our parents raised us. Parents who lived through the Great Depression clearly experienced the differences between luxuries and necessities. They tended to instill a strong work ethic in their children and pounded home the idea that life was uncertain and a constant struggle. Many baby boomers, on the other hand, adopted a quality-of-life focus. Their BMWs sported bumper stickers that proclaimed, "He Who Dies with the Most Toys Wins." In terms of parenting, this quality-of-life emphasis made baby boomers want to do everything possible for their children. Ironically, "doing everything" often meant doing it by proxy. Because the boomer lifestyle often called for parents to be at the office or on business trips, they ended up giving their children all sorts of things as substitutes for their physical presence.

The following story of two generations of a family illustrates how they were affected by and dealt with their affluence. Clearly, for them, affluence has become a double-edged sword.

A Parenting Generation Gap

Bob and Mary Smith were married in 1941. Shortly after Bob was drafted and fought in World War II, their twins, Peter and Elizabeth, were born in 1946. After the war, Bob took a job in sales with a Fortune 500 company while his wife stayed home. For the next ten years, he and Mary made ends meet only through conscientious budgeting. They bought a small house, and Peter and Elizabeth shared a bedroom until just before adolescence. Their financial fortunes took an upturn when Bob enjoyed a series of promotions at his corporation, and he eventually became a senior vice president. As the kids were growing up, they usually ate dinner together (Bob had to travel a bit at first, but his travel became much less frequent after the first five years with the company), and this became the best time for the family to share news of the day or discuss problems. The Smiths took a two-week summer vacation to the same rented house in the woods each year and attended church every Sunday. Television watching was restricted to weekends, and Bob and Mary closely monitored the children's homework.

Peter and Elizabeth began to receive a weekly allowance at age five and deposited the money in small piggy banks labeled "Save," "Charity," and "Fun." Their parents told them that they must divide their allowance equally among their three piggy banks. They could use the fun money as they wished (though Bob and Mary exercised veto power over excessive expenditures on candy and a few other items). At Christmas, the Charity bank would be emptied and the money given to the Salvation Army Santa Claus. The Save bank money could be used for special purchases (more expensive things the kids wanted), but again, Mary and Bob reserved their veto powers. If they did veto a purchase, however, they made an effort to communicate why the purchase would violate their values. For instance, once Bob explained that he would not let Elizabeth buy an expensive cashmere sweater because it was inappropriate for a twelve-year-old girl. Another time, Mary wouldn't let Peter buy a product from a company because she didn't agree with its employment practices (there had been a number of stories in the newspaper about their exploitive use of child labor).

Peter married Linda in 1971 at the age of twenty-five after graduating from law school. He got a job with a major law firm and began working as an associate, often spending seventy to eighty hours each week in the office. In 1974 they had their first son, and another boy followed three years later. One year after their second son was born, Linda went back to work as a real estate agent. Both Peter and Linda had found their dream house in a wonderful neighborhood, but to afford it, Linda needed to contribute to the family's income. She became very successful, and they hired an au pair to help with the kids. Peter was insistent that his sons have their own bedrooms as well as their own phones and televisions. In addition, each child was allowed to use his allowance as he saw fit. He told Linda that though he believed his parents had been fair with him and his sister, he thought they suffered from a depression-era mentality.

"After all," he said, "I'm making more than my father ever made, and you make a good salary. We should give our children every advantage."

Peter and Linda never talked to their children about money. Although his parents had routinely discussed the topic with him and Elizabeth and always answered their money questions, Peter and Linda both felt uncomfortable letting their children know how much money they made. It was almost as if they were embarrassed by their wealth. Once, their younger son asked them if they could give money to homeless people who were begging on the street, and Peter told his son that he was too young to understand why it wasn't a good idea.

Peter's two sons never got in serious trouble during their school years, but they were also indifferent to learning. Their grades were mediocre at best, and neither threats of punishment nor incentives (such as increased allowances) motivated them to get better grades. Perhaps even more significantly, they didn't seem interested in any subject, inside or outside of school. They hung around with a bunch of similarly below-average students, and as much as Peter and Linda tried to stimulate their interest in sports and music (two activities both Peter and Linda loved), they were met with indifference. Though their sons graduated from high school and went on to college, both eventually dropped out. The older son now has a job with Linda's real estate firm (though he constantly complains about it), and the younger one moves from job to job without finding anything he likes. Although they've matured somewhat since adolescence and the older one has married, they seem unhappy and uncertain about what to do with their lives.

Lessons Learned

Peter and Linda had a significantly different approach than Peter's parents to child raising. It's not that Peter and Linda were "bad" parents. To a certain extent, their parenting mistakes reflected cultural norms, and they were treating their children in ways that probably weren't much different from the ways other parents in their community raised their children. Nonetheless, they never seemed to really connect with their children in a meaningful way. They failed to provide them with bedrock values related to financial issues; they didn't instill a "money morality" in their children that would have helped combat the negative impact of affluence in their lives. Specifically, Peter and Linda

- turned money into a taboo subject
- gave their kids many things without making them accountable for what they received (or spent)

- never spent the time necessary talking to and being with their kids (in part because of their hectic work schedules) to communicate how goals, social responsibility, and meaningful work are all connected to affluence

SILVER NUGGET

Recall the last time you and your child talked about money. Think about what was said and what your position was. In hindsight, what do you feel your child took away from the discussion?

This education in values determines whether affluence has a positive or negative impact on children's development. Affluence isn't like tobacco; there's no need for a warning label stating that it is hazardous to a child's emotional health. It's mixing affluence with poor or no values that produces problems.

Your Money Narrative

Instilling the appropriate money values in a child is easier said than done. It's not as simple as sitting your child down and delivering a lecture about fiscal responsibility or about the importance of doing good in the world. Kids take their cues from thousands of interactions with you, from listening to what you say and observing what you do in a wide variety of situations. Many times, you won't even be aware of how you're influencing them. Therefore, the first thing you need to do is make your financial attitudes highly conscious. To that end, you and your spouse need to create a money narrative, a history of your relationship to financial issues. The following questions will help you create that narrative:

- What are two of your earliest money memories (e.g., the first important purchase you made)?
- What did you learn from your mother about money?
- What did you learn from your father about money?
- How did these parental messages affect you as you grew up?
- What are some of your family stories about money (the type of stories that are told when your immediate or extended family gets together—the time Dad was incredibly cheap or the big fight over Grandpa's will)?
- What did your mother or father or both do with their money that you particularly admired?
- What did they do with their money that you found offensive or unethical?
- What kind of financial education did you receive when you were growing up? Was it helpful? Would you change it in any way?
- What were the big emotional issues around money in your family when you were growing up? Are there any themes that persisted and still affect you today?
- Do your current attitudes and values about money differ from your parents' attitudes and values? Your siblings'? Your spouse's? If yes, how and why?
- How do you feel about your own affluence? What are the primary emotions that come to mind?
- What messages about money do you think you're sending to your children?

From your answers to these questions, create your money narrative—an open, honest, and personal story about the significant money attitudes and experiences in your life. Try to get in touch with what money means to you and how your attitudes toward it have developed over the years. We've found that it's often easier to figure out what your attitudes are if you put them in the form of a story. Take a moment to write your money story now because we're going to look at it again in Chapter 3.

We'll provide other, more focused tools later in the book to help you define your money relationships and the underlying values. For now, we'd simply like you to explore your feelings about money through this storytelling activity. Ideally, both you and your spouse will create narratives and share them with each other. Talk about what each story suggests. If Jack grew up in a stingy family, does he display the same stingy behavior or has he gone in the opposite direction and become a spendthrift? Or, like Barbara, who grew up in a wealthy family where no one ever gave to charities, is your spouse also reluctant to give money away to those in need?

If you simply think and talk about your money narratives, you'll have already increased the odds that affluence will be a friend rather than a foe in raising your children.

2

Keeping Your Child's Development on Track

To understand how and why affluence sometimes has a negative impact on children, we need to understand certain
aspects of developmental psychology. In the last fifty years, psychologists have learned a tremendous amount about the child-
development process. One of the truly crucial discoveries has been
the importance of children forming a secure attachment with
attachment figures while they are young. Without this bond, children tend to experience all sorts of emotional difficulties as they
go through different developmental stages.

What's instructive from our perspective is the impact of affluence on attachment. We've found that in upscale households
where there are attachment problems, kids are more likely to
exhibit the negative attitudes and behaviors discussed in the previous chapter. This is because affluence has been allowed to interfere with the children's ability to form a secure attachment and
thus prevents them from accomplishing a series of developmental
tasks as they grow. The good news is that affluence does not have
to interfere with your child developing a secure attachment and
growing up emotionally healthy. And if affluence has been
allowed to interfere, it's not too late to work on establishing a
secure relationship with your child. To help you understand this

concept, we'd like to begin by giving you a sense of what secure attachment entails. More details concerning attachment may be found in the Appendix.

Attachment Is Tough When There's No One There to Attach To

Just after the end of World War II, British psychoanalyst John Bowlby noted a marked increase in mental illness among young children who had been separated from their families and reared for prolonged periods in orphanages. Bowlby determined that it's crucial for young children to experience a warm, intimate, and continuous relationship with a caregiver in which both find satisfaction and enjoyment. Bowlby referred to this relationship as a "secure attachment" and called the caregivers "attachment figures."

The mother is not the only person who can serve as an attachment figure. Studies have shown no discernable difference in the quality of a child's secure attachment whether the mother or the father is the primary caregiver. In fact, children are capable of developing secure attachments with several adults. Nannies, grandparents, and day-care providers can all serve as attachment figures. The key is that the caregiver *be there*, both emotionally and physically, on a consistent basis.

Many psychologists believe that the nature of our attachment during our first few years of life has long-term psychological and emotional consequences. The quality of our attachment as young children universally affects the way we relate to the world as adults. If a young child forms a secure attachment, she learns to view her environment as safe. Because she is treated in a loving manner, she learns to react in an emotionally appropriate way. She cries if she is hungry, but she stops crying and is happy once she is fed and soothed. Psychologists refer to this type of appropriate emotional behavior as *self-regulation*. Children who have developed the capacity for self-regulation tend to exhibit increased emotional resilience when dealing with adversity and tend to do well in social relationships as they grow older.

A young child who fails to develop a secure attachment is not taught to view her environment as safe. In self-defense, she tends either to overregulate or underregulate her emotions. If she overregulates and maintains too tight control, she tends to become emotionally rigid or avoidant. If she underregulates, she does not learn to control her emotions and can become insecure and clingy. Insecurely attached children tend to have difficulty in social relationships throughout their lives. They can grow into adults who end up being overly needy at one extreme or overly avoidant at the other.

SILVER NUGGET

Take out your calendar and go through it day by day, searching for ways to add thirty minutes to one hour each day for your child by cutting back on some nonchild activity (come home earlier or go out for dinner less) and replacing it with a child-centered activity, such as reading or playing games.

What is important for our purposes is that a child who has an insecure attachment and views the world as hostile is likely to grow into an adult who projects that insecurity onto other important relationships, including his relationship with money. In Chapter 3 you are going to examine your relationship with money. As you read Chapter 3, you will find a remarkable parallel between our kids' need for a secure attachment and the importance of our kids developing a secure relationship with money.

How Affluence Can Unravel Attachment Threads

Some families are well-off because both parents work at time-intensive (often high-stress) jobs. As a result, they spend a great deal of time in the office or traveling. A number of our clients include women who went back to work almost immediately after they had a child. They felt they had no choice from either a financial or career perspective but to return to work. Other couples who are affluent because one spouse makes a great deal of money or through inherited wealth may also be away from home a great deal; they may travel, may be involved with charity work, or may have some other calling that requires them to be away from home for significant periods of time.

Can your children develop a secure attachment if you are with them for only limited periods of time? Interestingly, this same problem is faced by many low-income families, especially those with a single parent. The answer for both is the same: do the best you can to foster a secure attachment with your children during the time you have together. When you cannot be home, make certain that your children are with other caring, consistent adults who can serve as attachment figures, such as grandparents, nannies, and child-care providers. We are not suggesting that you delegate raising your children to someone else. You would not be reading this book if you were not a concerned parent. We are simply saying that when you are with your children, really be with them, attuned to their moods and needs, and when you are not available, make certain that you provide additional adult attachment figures.

What are the keys to a secure attachment? What are the qualities that enable a person to become an attachment figure? How do you help foster a secure attachment with your child? If your child is going to spend substantial time with nannies or other nonparental caregivers, what do you need to look for?

The first and perhaps most important quality is consistency: being there for the child on a consistent basis. If you cannot be a full-time parent, avoid frequent changes in nannies or day-care facilities with a high staff turnover rate. In either situation, your child will find it extremely difficult to view her world as safe and consistent. If you are considering a day-care facility or preschool, find one with a good child-to-adult staff ratio.

Next, make sure you or your caregiver is "tuned in" to your child's emotions and responds appropriately, especially to the nonverbal signals that an infant uses to communicate. Eye contact, facial expression, tone of voice, bodily gestures, and the timing and intensity of gestures are fundamentally important nonverbal signals. By being attuned to these signals, you or the caregiver engage in what psychologists refer to as "collaborative communication" with the child. Your child feels understood, and that sense of connecting with another person helps in the infant's development of social, emotional, and cognitive functioning.

An attachment figure must also be able to engage in two interrelated concepts: reflective dialogue and emotional communication. Although an infant's brain is capable of language and abstract thinking, neither capacity is developed at birth. Both are learned, in part through the process of reflective dialogue. You or the other attachment figure must not only be receptive to your child's verbal and nonverbal signals, but must also be able to feed them back to the child in such a way that it creates "meaning" for the child. In other words, you need to help your child understand

and label the emotion or feeling she is experiencing. In addition to reflecting back your child's feelings, an attachment figure needs to share in the positive, joyful aspects of the child's life while remaining emotionally connected during moments of uncomfortable emotion, such as anger or frustration. When the child is experiencing those emotions, an attachment figure soothes the child and helps her realize that she is not going to be emotionally abandoned. In this way, your child learns that many different emotions are experienced in the course of a relationship—some positive and some uncomfortable—and that whatever the emotional experience is, you or the other caregiver will be present to share the experience with her.

For more information about the complex subject of attachment theory and the need for secure attachment, we highly recommend *Attachment Across the Life Cycle*, edited by Parkes, Stevenson-Hinde, and Marris, which brings together in one volume the work of seventeen psychiatrists, psychologists, sociologists, and ethologists. Many of the articles contain extensive bibliographies. Robert Karen's *Becoming Attached* is another excellent source of information on attachment theory.

The Five Stages: Developing an Appreciation for How Money Affects Childhood Development

We frequently hear parents asking, "What should we do to prevent our money from harming our children?" There is no one answer. Instead, there are five, corresponding to five developmental stages. By understanding what these stages are and how affluence can interfere, we are better prepared to use our financial resources to help children develop in emotionally healthy ways.

Psychoanalyst Erik Erikson has identified various developmental stages that we pass through, each stage characterized by a particular conflict or crisis that must be resolved for our continued emotional growth. Erikson identified eight developmental stages that extend throughout our lives, as shown in the box below. Each requires us to resolve a conflict or crisis to move on to the next stage.

Erikson's Eight Stages

Age	Developmental Task
Birth to One Year	Trust
Two to Three Years	Autonomy
Four to Five Years	Initiative
Six to Puberty	Industry
Adolescence	Identity
Early Adulthood	Intimacy
Middle Adulthood	Generativity
Later Adulthood	Integrity

For our purposes here, we're only going to look at the first five stages. To move through these stages, your child needs two things: to feel loved and to feel a sense of competency, which we like to refer to as the "I can do" feeling. A secure attachment facilitates your child's movement through the developmental stages.

First Stage: Trust Versus Mistrust

This stage occurs during a child's first year. It's when an infant must develop trust in his environment. He must trust that his basic physical and emotional needs—food, shelter, clothing, and love—

will be provided. As you can see, a secure attachment is the sine qua non of this stage. It used to be a given that one parent—usually the mother—would devote him- or herself to this task. Assuming that the mother was herself psychologically healthy, the child would not only develop this essential trust, but would be ready to move on to the next stage of development.

If secure attachment doesn't occur during this stage, mistrust is likely to occur. When a child develops mistrust at this early age, he is likely to be suspicious of others and fearful of the future. We've worked with some couples who have not realized how critical it is to provide their infants with a secure attachment. They are good parents in the sense that they love their kids, are great with them when they do spend time together, and wouldn't consciously do anything that they felt was harmful. Many times, they are so caught up in their careers and the need to provide financial security for their children that they overlook this other type of security. During the first year of their children's lives, however, they need to help them form secure attachments, either with themselves or with someone else.

In the best of all possible worlds, at least one parent is financially able to be a full-time mother or father during the first year, and she or he takes joy in parenting and is able to provide loving, quality care for the infant. But for various reasons this ideal scenario may not be possible. Single parents may have no alternative but to work; both parents may have significant careers, or two incomes may be needed to maintain the family's standard of living; the parents may be independently wealthy but are involved in community or other activities that require their full-time attention; or perhaps neither parent wants to stay home full-time. In all of these situations, some other adult, loving caregiver must be consistently available as an attachment figure when neither parent is home.

The following behaviors are indicative of parents who are failing to build a secure attachment:

- Not spending significant amounts of time with a child each day during the first year; a parent or other caregiver who doesn't see the child at all for days at a time
- A lack of emotional engagement when holding or feeding the child; a parent or other caregiver who constantly feels preoccupied and distracted when with the child
- Too much stimulation of the infant; a parent or other caregiver who doesn't respond to the baby's nonverbal cues, such as looking away, that mean the baby needs some space
- Having a high turnover of help or placing the child in a daycare center that is experiencing a high turnover

SILVER NUGGET

Practice focusing completely and absolutely on your child as if you were practicing some form of meditation. Block out all other thoughts and distractions and be with your child in the moment.

Second Stage: Autonomy Versus Shame and Doubt

The goal for a two- to three-year-old child is to establish a sense of separateness from his parents and start becoming a self-sufficient and autonomous individual. Obviously, children are still dependent on parents at this age, but they also have the opportunity to do some things on their own, such as feeding, walking, and talking. Toilet training begins at age two to three for many children, and their proud declaration, "Mommy, look at what I can do," is a sign of autonomy. When children aren't allowed to establish a certain measure of self-sufficiency at this age, however, they often experience self-esteem problems later in their lives as well as shame and doubt about their own abilities.

Affluence can breed overprotectiveness. Many parents tell us about how they try to "protect our kids from what we went through." When kids are two, this attitude may mean saying and doing things that prevent them from doing anything on their own. "Wait for me or you'll hurt yourself" is a common cry of overprotective parents. In other instances, kids' development can be stunted by what we call the "nanny shadow." Nannies and other employed helpers don't want parents to blame them if a child under their care skins a knee or has some other type of accident. As a result, they don't let kids take minor, acceptable risks: going down a slide by themselves or exploring their natural environment (playing with dirt, worms, etc.).

Signs of parents who are preventing natural development at this stage include the following:

- Unwillingness to let a child try challenging tasks or rushing in to help, saying things like, "You're too young to do that" or "I'll do it"
- Preventing a child from taking minor risks out of overblown fears of injury, infection, or tears
- Permitting nannies and other help to oversupervise a child and not allow that child the exploratory freedom he requires

Third Stage: Initiative Versus Guilt

From ages four to five, children are in the Initiative Stage. During this stage, they begin to discover what kind of people they're going to be. As they learn to work through simple puzzles and play with others, they start initiating activities of various sorts on their own. In the process, they learn to persevere and experience a sense of accomplishment.

If children are given the freedom and opportunity to initiate play activities, they will develop a strong sense of initiative. Children at this stage can hold conversations and their sense of initiative is strengthened if their parents treat their questions with respect. On the other hand, if a child is made to feel that his play activities are silly and his questions are a nuisance, he may develop a sense of guilt and inadequacy that will persist throughout later life.

Children in this stage are beginning to comprehend that other people have different ways of viewing the world. They are starting to develop a sense of compassion.

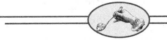

SILVER NUGGET

Engage your child in discussions about characters in a book, TV program, or movie. Ask her what the characters might be thinking and feeling.

Kids are now beginning to talk about beliefs. You can engage your child in discussion of "things of the mind"—ideas, attitudes, and opinions. Ask him what he thinks about things. Share with him what you think. Expose him to a diversity of ideas and experiences. You are exploring how your child thinks and giving him an opportunity to explore your mind.

Later, we discuss the important role that philanthropy plays in raising emotionally healthy children and look at the need for your children to understand socioeconomic diversity. At this age, your children are starting to develop the skills necessary to deal with these concepts.

This is also the time when children begin to develop a sense of right and wrong. As they *do* things on their own, they discover that some things are hurtful and shouldn't be done and some things are helpful and should be done.

Contradictory behaviors can harm children at this stage. Parents may preach good values—it's bad to hit, it's good to share, it's important to tell the truth—but they don't practice these values. We know more than one highly paid professional who talks about fairness and treating people equally yet looks down her nose at the handyman and cleaning lady or screams on the phone at a subordinate who didn't complete an assignment correctly. Or the child hears Dad "lie" to a friend, telling him he has an appointment and can't make lunch (and the child sees that Dad doesn't have an appointment). Or both parents talk about the importance of moderation and philanthropy yet the child sees them constantly purchasing expensive items and never experiences them giving money to charity. Kids can become confused by this contradictory behavior, and they shy away from initiating because of this confusion. Instead, they can become passive and feel guilty for what they haven't done.

Common signs of parents who may be preventing their children from successfully passing through this developmental stage include the following:

- Saying one thing but doing something else, creating value confusion in kids
- Unwillingness to let children initiate many things on their own, an extension of the overprotectiveness of the previous stage

- Being overly hard on children when they try new things, causing them to feel guilty when they make mistakes and reluctant to initiate activities
- Rushing in to solve problems when the kid is frustrated. Instead, parents need to teach kids how to deal with frustration because it is inherent in the learning process

Fourth Stage: Industry Versus Inferiority

Starting at age six or so, children enter school and reach the point where play is no longer a completely satisfying way of spending their time. They begin to want to feel useful, to want to make things through diligence and attention, and to achieve their potential. School requires children to play communally in complex games as well as achieve through their own efforts. For the first time, their development is dependent on interactions with others.

Affluent parents may create problems at this stage if they don't encourage their child's efforts to do things for himself, and the concomitant lessons of earning, saving, and delaying gratification that earning one's own money provides. Some parents remove incentives for their children to make a little money through a lemonade stand or another endeavor to buy a desired toy. "You don't have to do that," Mom or Dad says. "We'll give you the money for the toy." Contrast that attitude with the following.

The eight-year-old son of a single mother we know asked for a computer in his bedroom. His mother said that it wasn't in the budget but offered to match anything he earned. He started a neighborhood car-washing business that he called The BuBBles Company. His older brother helped him produce advertising leaflets, and he soon had regular customers. Within a few months he had earned enough that, with Mom's matching funds, he could purchase the computer.

Activities such as this one or cookie sales or raking leaves promote a child's experience as a competent individual. This stage continues through puberty. When kids have difficulty with this developmental stage, the result is usually feelings of inadequacy and inferiority.

Affluence can become problematic from a developmental point of view because kids begin comparing themselves to their classmates during this stage. As a result of this comparison, children may begin to doubt the importance of industry in achieving goals. For instance, if kids feel that they have a nicer home and more toys than their classmates, they may develop a sense of privilege that inhibits their sense of industry. In other words, when so many things are given to them, they believe they don't have to work hard to achieve them. Parents who (consciously or not) communicate a privileged or even superior status do their children a disservice. Some kids who heed this message and don't work particularly hard in school end up receiving poor marks or negative teacher comments. As a result, they start to feel inadequate and inferior, even though they may paradoxically exhibit a superior attitude.

On the other hand, affluence used appropriately can be very positive during the industry stage. Tutoring and individualized instruction can be of great assistance to the child. As parents, we simply need to avoid using our affluence to take away our children's struggle. Children who are not permitted to struggle and succeed often develop a sense of inferiority.

Signs of parents who may be causing their children problems during this developmental stage include the following:

- Bragging about how much they have compared to others
- Obsessing about acquiring things, especially the best of everything—in other words, a focus on the external rather than the internal

- Reassuring children constantly that they "don't need to worry" because "we have plenty"
- Being too busy to maintain interest in the child's schoolwork
- Setting goals for the child without regard for what the child wants
- Doing homework for the child (or having tutors do it) when the child is frustrated
- Buying children whatever they want

Fifth Stage: Identity Versus Role Confusion

In adolescence, children are developing "ego identity." This means knowing who they are, identifying their social roles, and being comfortable with that knowledge. It comes down to feeling that they are learning to master life successfully. When they fail to develop this identity, teenagers feel they must conform to others' expectations or that they must rebel against those expectations. In either case, these failures result in "identity diffusion," or a sense that they just can't take hold of life.

Although parents in all income groups may find themselves with role-confused adolescents, the problem is sometimes more acute in affluent households because of the increased number of choices and opportunities facing your child. As you might imagine, it's difficult for kids to develop a sense of identity if the following questions are continuously running through their minds:

- Do people like me for myself or for my family's money?
- Who am I without my family's money?
- Will I be able to survive without my family's money?
- How can I be as successful as my parents?

It's very easy for teenagers to believe that their friends like them only because they have a swimming pool or because they have season tickets for games played by their city's top sports team. They may also have this gnawing, unarticulated fear that their worth as human beings is directly tied to the family's net worth. They may not be able to envision how they'll survive when they leave home and are on their own and who they'll be in this new environment. Although some rebellion during adolescence is natural, role-confused adolescents not only do poorly in school, but are vulnerable to drug and alcohol abuse and tend to be friends with equally confused kids.

Signs of parents who are contributing to this confusion rather than aiding identity formation include the following:

- Unwillingness to talk to kids honestly and openly about money and values
- Overindulgence that unconsciously links individual and financial worth in a child's mind
- Measuring adult achievements solely in financial terms (rather than in job satisfaction, meaningful work, etc.)

SILVER NUGGET

What developmental stage is your child passing through? What are his tasks? How can you help in a constructive manner?

Taking the Right Developmental Steps

Unfortunately, there's no magic formula for parents who want to create a strong attachment bond with their child and facilitate the developmental process. We would not presume to recommend that all mothers or fathers should stay home with their children through adolescence and make attachment their number-one priority. Nor would we suggest that there's only one way for parents to help their children navigate adolescence or to take care of a baby, for that matter.

What we've found to be most effective for affluent parents, however, is being aware of attachment and development issues and using this top-of-mind awareness to avoid the traps to which they're most vulnerable. The following guide will help you do just that.

Attachment

Spend emotional time with your child rather than just task time. We've found that parents who work at high-stress, high-powered jobs make an effort to be with their children, but sometimes they're only half there. They change their children's diapers, accompany them to activities, and talk and listen to them, but their attention is divided. As a result, the child doesn't feel connected with the parent; there's no empathetic listening or complete, wholehearted involvement in play. Kids sense this emotional distance, and it can make attachment difficult. Be more than a dutiful parent.

Trust Versus Mistrust

Be there when you are there. If you are a full-time parent, recognize that parenting is a full-time job. If you are home only before and after work hours, make certain that you provide the child with an attachment figure and spend as much time with your children as you can. Remember, the nanny or other caregiver who helps take care of your children may be a wonderful attachment figure, but she still isn't your children's parent. You are. You could be crawling around on the floor playing with toys; you could be singing lullabies; you need to be watching and cheering as she makes funny sounds and faces; you could be spooning baby food into her mouth. During the first year, one parent may decide to make some sacrifices from a work or a social activity perspective, but it's worth it to participate in your child's first year of life and help your child develop trust.

Autonomy Versus Shame and Doubt

Give your child opportunities. Encourage him to try new things and be supportive if he has trouble with them at first. Certainly you want to prevent your child from doing anything that might put him in any kind of physical danger, but you also want to give him a great deal of freedom to explore his environment and experiment with it. One of the advantages of affluence in this regard is that you can provide him with all sorts of challenging games, trips, and adventures that will allow him to become autonomous.

Initiative Versus Guilt

Live your values. Be consistent in what you say and do as your child observes you. At this stage of his life, your child is going to be initiating all sorts of activities, and you want him to understand that it's important to live his life according to his beliefs. Begin to talk to your child about his ideas and opinions. Be especially aware of how you behave relative to the affluence-related issues we've discussed. If you preach equality, do you treat the hired help as a servant or with the respect of an equal? If you feel snobbery is abhorrent, do you make snide comments about the neighbors' secondhand cars or bad taste in clothes?

Industry Versus Inferiority

Keep your wealth in perspective. You need to communicate that money isn't everything. In various ways, you should help your kids understand that money isn't a magical thing that confers happiness, health, fame, and achievement on those who have it. Try to focus on your children's internal qualities as opposed to their external ones. Your kids will usually respond by being industrious at school, recognizing that there are rewards in individual hard work and achievement and that not everything will be given to them. The key to this stage is for your child to develop internal motivation.

Identity Versus Role Confusion

Talk to your children honestly and openly about money and communicate that the family money won't save or support them. Kids must learn that, as adults, they're on their own and that they're going to need their own identities to be on their own. Talk honestly and openly about family money. If they have questions about their inheritance, answer them. They need to see that affluence is a privilege that has to be earned and that the first step in earning it is developing a singular identity—an identity that will allow them to create a place for themselves in whatever field they choose. Guide them in identifying and developing passions in life.

SILVER NUGGET

Pay attention to what makes your child's eyes light up with excitement, no matter how outrageous it seems.

Remember that as children move through these stages, they need to feel loved and they need to feel competent. As affluent parents, be careful not to overshadow your child with your own success.

Tell your child about some of your mistakes and some of your failures. In this way you can help her understand that rejection and failure are parts of life.

Help your child develop her own "I can do" mindset as she moves through the developmental stages, dealing with struggles, failures, and successes, while feeling loved and secure.

3

Money Personalities

In the first chapter, we asked you to think about your feelings about and experiences with money so that you could obtain a sense of how you have related to money throughout your life. If you did this, you probably have an inkling of your relationship with money and some personality traits that emanate from that relationship. In this chapter we want to help you become aware of what that relationship entails and how this awareness can help you parent in a psychologically healthy way as your child develops.

Let's start with a short quiz that can help you begin to identify some of your money relationships. Jot down your answers on a piece of paper and save it. We'll look at your answers a bit later in this chapter.

1. **I get the greatest pleasure out of**
   a. making money
   b. spending money
   c. managing money
   d. saving money
   e. investing money

2. **With which statement do you most identify?**
   a. To me, money is a problem. I often think of money as the root of all evil.

b. To me, money is a scorecard. The more I make, the higher I score.

c. All work and no play makes Jack a dull boy.

3. **With which statement do you most agree?**
   a. Because I can't take it with me, I like to spend it now.
   b. A penny saved is a penny earned.
   c. I save some, spend some, and give some to charity.

4. **Which statement describes you the best?**
   a. I carefully review statements from my bank or broker when I receive them.
   b. I tend to procrastinate when it comes to paying bills or doing my taxes and sometimes have to pay late charges or penalties.
   c. I probably could keep better records, but I'm always able to find what I need, and my bills get paid on time.

We'll look at your answers a little later in this chapter.

The Elements of a Money Personality

We all have very specific money personalities. As a parent, you should know the emotional and psychological themes attached to your money relationships. The way you think and feel about money influences the way you behave around money and can have a tremendous impact on your children.

Theodore Millon, a professor of psychiatry at Harvard University and the University of Miami, defines personality as a pattern of deeply embedded and broadly exhibited cognitive (how we think), affective (how we feel), and behavioral (what we do) traits that persist over time. A money personality, therefore, is the sum of what we think, feel, and do relative to money.

As the result of our money personalities, money is meaningful to people on different levels and in different ways. For some people, money is a source of security or freedom; for others, it's a cause of anxiety or dependence. There are also those who have terrible guilt over spending money and are terrified of not having enough. Money certainly can have positive themes; some associate money with stewardship and see it as a means to a noble end.

Each of us develops a unique relationship with money in three separate dimensions: acquisition, use, and management. We develop this three-dimensional relationship largely as the result of two factors: the messages we receive during childhood about money and values and the way we organize this information in our minds.

We process and organize these money messages, as well as our behaviors around money, in very individualistic ways. Even siblings in the same household are likely to organize their views and their relationships with money very differently.

Bob and Sherry are thirty-two-year-old twins who grew up in a household where the father made all of the money decisions. Both were constantly exposed to their mother deferring to their money-dominant father, yet when Bob and Sherry grew up, they manifested very different money personalities. While Bob replicated his father's behaviors and married a woman who deferred to him on financial matters, Sherry established a more egalitarian relationship in which she and her spouse shared financial decision making equally.

Bob and Sherry organized and processed their money messages differently. Although some of this occurs on an unconscious level, some of it can be done very consciously. What will help you consciously shape your parenting behaviors in positive ways is understanding the three dimensions of money relationships.

A useful way of looking at these three relationships is to think of the ruler shown on page 40.

Three dimensions of money relationships.

The center portion of the ruler represents a secure relationship with one of the three dimensions of money. The ends of the ruler each represent different types of insecure relationships in which people have difficulty regulating their money behavior. We like to use a ruler to illustrate the concept because it allows you to see that there is a range of normal relationships with money in each dimension, as well as a range of insecure relationships. The borders between secure and insecure can be fuzzy and are different with practically everyone. We cannot draw a line in the sand and say that everyone on this side of the line is secure and everyone on the other side is insecure.

When your money relationship in one of the dimensions is normal or secure, two tests are being met: (1) your relationship in that dimension will not get you into money trouble and (2) you are reasonably content with the relationship. You might want to be more organized or earn or save a bit more or spend a little less, but, all things considered, the situation is acceptable. When you have an insecure relationship in one of the money dimensions, that relationship has either already gotten you into money trouble or it may someday. And, for most people, an insecure relationship with money is a psychic drain, causing them anxiety. Some people, however, have an insecure relationship with money but view it as a natural and inevitable part of their lives. They take their money problems for granted. At the extreme ends of the ruler we find people whose relationship with money is so abnormal that it can correctly be viewed as pathological. These are people with adequate to high incomes who lose their homes because they don't pay their bills or go to prison for tax evasion or securities fraud.

Each of us tends to have different degrees of security or insecurity when dealing with the three dimensions of acquisition, use, and management. For each of us, one or two of these dimensions tends to be more important than the others or other. This occurs either because your relationship in that dimension is secure and successful or insecure and problem laden. Even if all of your money relationships are reasonably secure, you are likely to find that one dimension is more important to you than the others. If you are a successful entrepreneur and your goal in life is creating and selling new businesses, acquisition is likely to be more important to you than either use or management. There is nothing wrong or abnormal if one relationship is more important than the others. The mere fact that you favor acquisition over use or management does not, by itself, imply that you have taken that relationship to such an extreme that it approaches a form of pathology. How you implement that relationship—how your acquisition behaviors play out in the real world, for instance—determines the normality of that money relationship.

Let's look at each of the three relationships in more detail.

• **Money Acquisition:** This is the dimension that relates to how you get money. Most of us tend to be somewhere in the middle of the ruler; we neither fear money nor are we prepared to break the law to acquire more. As we move toward either end, we find people who either overregulate or underregulate their behavior with money. On one end of the ruler, you have the avoidant, or overregulator. This person views money as the root of all evil. At the other end, you have the insatiable, or underregulator, the white-collar criminal who will break any law and bend any rule to acquire more and more, for whom acquiring money is the source of all happiness. A wonderful example of an insatiable is John D. Rockefeller. At the time when he was the wealthiest man in the world, he was asked by a reporter, "How much money is enough?" His answer: "Just a little bit more."

If you treat acquisition as a ruler, it would look like this:

| INSECURE (avoidant) | SECURE | INSECURE (insatiable) |

Money acquisition ruler.

• **Money Use:** This is the dimension of how you save or spend. Again, most of us are in the middle, being reasonably careful and conscious of our use of money. On one end, you have the miser, or overregulator, of which Hetty Green is one of America's best-known examples. Born in 1834 into a wealthy New England family, she inherited $7.5 million dollars at age twenty-one. Through careful investing, she built her inheritance into a Wall Street fortune worth more than $100 million by the time of her death in 1916. The October 1998 edition of *American Heritage* ranks Green as thirty-sixth out of the forty richest Americans in history. Expressed in today's dollars, her fortune had a buying power estimated at $17.3 billion. Yet Green's penny-pinching was truly pathological. In one infamous incident, her refusal to pay for medical care for her fifteen-year-old son resulted in the eventual amputation of his leg! At the other end of the ruler is the compulsive overspender. This is a person who underregulates, who has no boundaries when it comes to using money.

If you look at use as a ruler, it would look like this:

INSECURE (miser)	SECURE	INSECURE (compulsive overspender)

Money use ruler.

• **Money Management:** This is how you handle money. It includes everything from paying bills to managing your investment portfolio. Some of these functions are often delegated to professional advisors. On one end, you have the obsessive-compulsive who overregulates by micromanaging down to the last dime. At the other end, you have the chaotic, or underregulated, individual, who is extremely disorganized or procrastinates in paying bills to such an extent that his or her credit is often ruined.

If you look at management as a ruler, it would look like this:

INSECURE (micromanager)	SECURE	INSECURE (chaotic)

Money management ruler.

Working on Your Money-Related Behavior

Now that you understand the three dimensions of money relationships, let's take a look at the quiz at the start of this chapter.

The first question asked you to determine which of the three dimensions was most important to you. If you circled *(a)*, you're into acquisition. Selecting *(b)* or *(d)* means that use is important to you. And choosing *(c)* or *(e)* means that management is the most important dimension for you.

Question 2 focused on acquisition. If you selected *(a)*, your relationship with acquisition tends toward the avoidant side of the spectrum. Selecting *(b)* puts you toward the insatiable side, and *(c)* places you somewhere in the secure middle section.

Question 3 looked at use. Choosing *(a)* means that your approach to use probably tends toward the compulsive, over-spender side; selecting *(b)* puts you more toward the miser side. Choosing *(c)* again places you somewhere in the secure middle section.

Question 4 dealt with management. If you selected *(a)*, you probably tend toward the micromanager side of the spectrum. Selecting *(b)* places you toward the chaotic side. Once again, *(c)* puts you somewhere in the middle.

There are four things to keep in mind as you determine your money relationships in each of the three dimensions.

First, it is important not to treat the dividing lines between secure and insecure relationships as fixed and clear. There is room for a wide range of secure behaviors. The difference between secure and insecure is a combination of emotions (are you content or anxious about the relationship?) and finances (will the relationship get you into money trouble?). Thus, if the quiz shows that you tend toward one end of the relationship spectrum or the other, your relationship is not necessarily insecure. It may well fall within the broad range of secure behaviors.

Second, it's best if you and your spouse work on this together. If you both become aware of your money relationships, you can

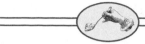

Silver nugget

Try to think of three people you know whose behaviors are extreme in terms of acquisition, use, and management. Then think about whether they are happy or not. Are their children well-adjusted?

start not only changing both your behaviors and the messages about money sent to your kids, but you can make sure you're not sending mixed messages.

Third, determining how your money behaviors affect your children is not an exact science. If you and your spouse are both insecure in the management dimension, this doesn't mean you're going to raise an absentminded professor who's always misplacing his checkbook. If you and your spouse are both secure in the area of acquisition, that doesn't guarantee that your child will grow up to be a billionaire. Every child is a unique combination of heredity and environment, and although you certainly can influence your child's relationship with money, you can't control all the factors. We do know, however, that there is a definite correlation between the messages parents send their kids and how those messages are translated into behaviors as children mature. In Eileen's study on the impact of sudden wealth, close to 90 percent of children who received early money messages stressing the importance of saving and spending responsibly exhibited these positive behaviors as adults. But not all of these children exhibited such behaviors when they were kids. Although the messages were vitally important, their impact sometimes did not emerge until the kids became adults.

Fourth, we've found that parents who make the effort to understand the root of their own money behaviors are more likely to have a positive influence on their children's behaviors than parents who do not. Greater understanding of why they acquire, use, and manage money the way they do translates into greater impact on their children's regulation of their money behaviors in the three dimensions of acquisition, use, and management of money.

With that in mind, the following six-step process will help you understand the root of your money attitudes.

Step One: Compare Your Past and Present Experiences with Money

In Chapter 1 we asked you to create your money narrative. If you wrote it down, you might want to read it over now. Then answer the following questions:

1. Describe the emotional climate surrounding your current relationship with money. Is it marked by anxiety, guilt, pride, and other feelings?
2. Think about your childhood and describe the emotional climate around money in your home.
3. Are the past and present similar or different? If different, in what ways do they differ?

Step Two: Try This Exercise

Take a blank piece of paper and create a chart that looks like the one at the top of page 47.

ACQUISITION	Avoidant	Secure	Insatiable
USE	Miser	Secure	Compulsive Overspender
MANAGEMENT	Micromanager	Secure	Chaotic

Step Three: Rate Yourself in All Three Dimensions

Using the chart, rate yourself in the three dimensions. If you are married or have a significant other, rate yourselves and then rate each other. If the two of you disagree, this provides a wonderful impetus for a dialogue about the hows and whys of your money relationships.

Alan and Marisa attended one of our presentations and subsequently wrote us:

> We've been meeting almost every morning for fifteen to thirty minutes to review the previous day using these three lenses of acquisition, use, and management. I can't tell how many valuable insights we've discovered through this process. And often the question arises, Why did we do that? Or why did I do that? Or, when we're feeling most comfortable with each other, why did you do that?

For most people, one of the dimensions is more important than the other two. In many instances, the predominant dimension correlates with the person's chosen profession. Entrepreneurs tend to emphasize acquisition, financial consultants concentrate on use, and accountants tend to stress management. Which dimension is the most important for you: acquisition, use, or management? The fact that one dimension may be more important to you than the others is part of your money personality.

Step Four: Consider the Messages You're Sending

Based on your relationships in each of the three dimensions, you're sending money messages to your children. Answer the following questions to determine what those messages are:

1. Looking back on how you've acted and talked about money issues in front of your children, what messages do you think you're sending them?
2. What messages do you think your spouse is sending your children?
3. If you believe you and your spouse have significantly different relationships with money, do you think your behaviors are sending mixed messages to your kids?

Step Five: Compare Your Charts with Others

Create money relationship charts for your parents and siblings just as you did for yourself. As you do so, answer the following questions:

1. Describe the kind of messages your parents sent you about money; what was the impact of those messages on you?
2. Did your siblings mentally organize these parental messages in the same way that you did, resulting in similar money personalities? Or are their personalities different?
3. Compare your parents' relationship charts to your own. How are these relationships similar to yours and how are they different? Are your money relationships a combination of those of your parents or are they different?

Step Six: Create a Money Genogram

A *genogram*, a specialized form of a family tree used in psychology, will enable you to see family patterns in money relationships. Before putting a genogram together, here are some useful symbols that will make this activity easier:

☐ Males are represented by a square.
○ Females are represented by a circle.

Marriage is represented by male and female connected with a solid line. If two people are living together but not married, use a dotted line to connect the male and female. Divorce is shown by a double slash through the marriage line.

Children are indicated by a vertical line descending from the marriage line and terminating in a circle or a square.

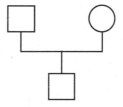

If someone is deceased, place an X inside of the person's square or circle.

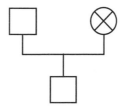

Here is a genogram for Mary and George, a couple who married, had two children (Sam and Cynthia), and divorced. George then married Janet, and they had one more child (Emily). Their genogram looks like this:

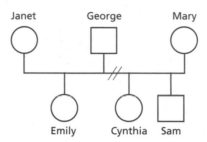

Now that you have the basics of the genogram, the key is to designate the dominant money relationships. Insert an *A* (Acquisition), *U* (Use), or *M* (Management) in the appropriate circle or square. Next, add either a plus sign to show the relationship is secure (*A*+) or a minus sign to show that it's insecure (*A*−); remember that a relationship is dominant either because it represents a secure and successful part of a person's life or because it's a source of insecurity and anxiety. It's possible that someone might have two dominant relationships: one area where he's secure and successful and another where he's insecure and anxious. If this is the case, insert both letters and accompany each with a plus or minus sign (e.g., *U*+ and *M*−).

With all this in mind, create a money genogram for your family. Start with you and your spouse, add your parents and spouse's parents, and then your children. Designate the money relationship for all family members with a letter and plus or minus sign (you can do this with children if they're "tweens," in that in-between stage, or teens and sometimes even when they're younger). If you feel it's relevant, include your siblings in the genogram.

When you're done, identify the patterns that jump out at you.

Bringing a Genogram to Life (and Money Relationships to Paper)

Elizabeth and Jack are a married couple in their early fifties. Jack is a successful plastic surgeon, and Elizabeth is an interior designer. They enjoy a high standard of living, including annual vacations to Europe, a beautiful home, and expensive cars. Married for twenty-eight years, they have a twenty-four-year-old son, Justin. Elizabeth and Jack have become increasingly concerned about Justin. His spending habits have spiraled out of control, and they recently had to bail him out after he maxed out his credit cards on a vacation he took with some friends. Although Justin had overspent in the past, his parents believe that he is old enough to know better.

Creating a money genogram helped all three of them become more aware of their money relationships. Although it would have been preferable if they did this genogram years ago, they still reaped benefits by creating a family money tree at this late date. One of their most important discoveries was that though financial anxiety was a theme that ran through three generations of their family, each family member organized that anxiety differently. Jack, for instance, grew up in a well-to-do household where his father made a good living, but his mother frequently expressed the concern that "someday we won't have enough." As an adult, Jack's primary relationship with money is use, and although he tends toward the overspender end of the use continuum—he spends liberally on expensive toys such as computers, cameras, and cars—he mentally beats himself up when the bills arrive and panics, feeling like he's spending way too much.

Elizabeth's father died when she was a child, and the family lifestyle changed dramatically at that point. Elizabeth remembers her mother sitting at the dining room table, shuffling bills and trying to make ends meet. For years, a familiar and dreaded scene was her mother puffing away on a cigarette, a tortured look on her face and her hands tightly clasping one bill or another. As an adult, Elizabeth's primary relationship with money is management, and she's highly insecure and disorganized when it comes to paying bills on time.

Interestingly, Justin reacted to his mother's chaotic management style by taking the opposite approach to management. His checkbook is always perfectly balanced, and he becomes very upset if there's a discrepancy of even a few cents. At the same time, he is even more of an overspender than his father, but unlike his father, there is a good reason for the anxiety he feels; he's spending more than he has.

This is what their genogram looks like:

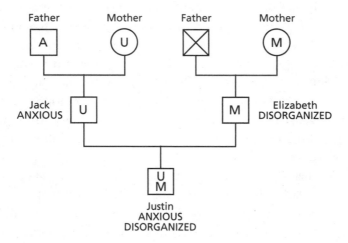

Preparing their genogram was eye-opening for everyone, but especially for Justin. He never realized the patterns of how money was used and managed. He saw how he had accepted his father's relationship with use but that he was in no position to spend money the way his father did. Just as important, he recognized how his management style was a reaction to his mother's management style. This knowledge helped him feel better about himself and start taking responsibility for his behaviors. As you can see, a genogram can help describe both money behaviors and the emotional roots of those behaviors.

Changing Money Relationships

The primary goal of understanding your relationships with money is awareness. The more you and your spouse are aware of your primary money relationships, the more able you'll be to adjust those relationships. The better you understand the root of these relationships, the better you'll be at analyzing and talking about why you behave the way you do. As a general rule, parents who are aware of their relationships with money raise children who are comfortable with their own money relationships. We've found that these parents are much less likely to have kids who exhibit negative behaviors and attitudes: a sense of entitlement, lack of ambition, and so on.

Why this is so may involve a variety of factors, but the main one is that these parents can regulate their money behaviors to moderate or eliminate the negative impact. They can hone in on the specific area—use, acquisition, or management—where they have money relationship problems and attempt to regulate their behavior accordingly. Sometimes this adjustment is as simple as refraining from mentioning worries about not having enough money around their children; sometimes it requires both spouses to agree that they'll work together to manage their money in ways that are organized and logical; sometimes it's more complicated, and parents need to seek therapy to deal with deep-seated fears or other issues that make them extremely insecure in a given money dimension.

Even in this last case it's possible for people to make profound psychological shifts that lead to new (and better) ways of passing on healthy attitudes toward money. We have a sixty-five-year-old friend who, for most of her life, was insecure in the use dimension. Though she lived well, she was quite frugal, and as she got older, she became obsessed with creating an estate plan that would maximize the amount of money her children would receive. This obsession not only irritated her husband, but strained the relationship with her adult children, who felt she was denying herself many pleasurable experiences because she insisted on giving them the largest amount of money possible. Her psychological shift had probably been building incrementally through a number of experiences, but one day she was sitting in her attorney's office and noticed a framed needlepoint sampler on the wall that said, "Fly First Class—Your Heirs Will."

The sampler triggered her psychological shift. From that point on, she decided to spend more on herself and leave a large percentage of her estate to charity. It suddenly sank in that her children were successful and would do fine no matter what she left them and that she could use her money in ways that made more sense.

We relate this story not to suggest that you are likely to undergo an epiphany in your lawyer's office, but to demonstrate that it's possible for anyone to change deep-seated money behaviors. Typically, parents change their behaviors more gradually, less dramatically, but no less effectively. Below are some of the ways we've found that will help you change your relationship with money.

Therapy

If you are seriously concerned about your relationship with money, you should consider working with a therapist specializing in the psychology of money. Many parents wait to seek therapy—either for themselves or their children or all of them—until their kids get in trouble. Often, this happens when the children are adolescents. Not all therapists are trained to address the specific link between money behaviors and child raising, yet they do encourage parents to explore the roots of a child's problems, and a link is often made with parental behaviors.

Leon, for instance, is a forty-four-year-old divorced father of two teenagers. Leon shares joint custody of the children, though they live with his ex-wife. As a highly successful entrepreneur, Leon is doing well; he has been astute in buying and selling a number of businesses. As committed as Leon is to his entrepreneurial path, he also makes time for charitable work and is heavily involved in local nonprofit organizations that work to help disadvantaged children.

When his older son, Brian, turned sixteen, Leon bought him a Porsche. This was typical of Leon's behavior toward both of his kids; he bought them expensive toys when they were little and continued this practice throughout the years. In the year after receiving the Porsche, Brian was arrested twice, once for reckless driving and the second time for driving under the influence. These and other incidents alarmed Leon and he sought therapy to deal with his growing anxiety about Brian. During the sessions, Leon began to see how his intense focus on being an entrepreneur (his primary money relationship was acquisition) affected his children. His various business deals occupied a great deal of time and travel, and even when Leon was still married, he wasn't home much. When he was with his children, he frequently talked to them about his "big deals," and they often saw him talking on his cell phone with business associates. Because he didn't pay much attention to his children, he felt guilty and bought them things in compensation.

In talking with the therapist, he came to realize that he was only sharing one part of himself with his kids, that he was bombarding them with his acquisitive side. Amazingly, his children weren't even aware that he was involved in charitable work. Over the years, Brian had become increasingly angry about how his father tried to buy his love with gifts rather than attention. As much as Brian enjoyed having a cool car, part of him was also furious at his father. At some level he knew that the car was a substitute for love and attention, and he expressed his anger by driving it recklessly.

Leon began changing his behaviors toward his children in part because of therapy. Of course, a good deal of damage had already been done. As the previous chapter pointed out, these money issues need to be addressed early on, and many therapeutic interventions happen later rather than sooner. Still, they can be a very effective tool for parents interested in understanding how they may have contributed to their children's problems and how to change their money behaviors accordingly.

Dialogue

Talking with your spouse about your money relationships and how they might affect (or have affected) your children is an obvious and effective approach. Still, many parents rarely talk to each other about their money relationships. Either they don't find them relevant from a parenting perspective or they're not even aware of what these relationships entail.

Although talking doesn't solve problems in and of itself, it can lead to solutions. One spouse can make the other aware that he's setting a bad example for the children with his constant fretting about the family's financial resources. A couple can also use the tools and techniques in this chapter, addressing their primary money relationships and their genograms. We've found that these conversations raise awareness of the connection between money behaviors and how a child develops.

It's important that these conversations not be about blame. Just about everyone has some issue with money, and to castigate your spouse for being an obsessive manager of money is unproductive. Here are some tips for talking with your spouse:

- Talk about behaviors in nonjudgmental ways. For example, say, "I see that you don't seem to like all the paperwork involved in handling our medical insurance" rather than "We're losing hundreds of dollars because you're too disorganized to submit our medical insurance forms on time." Accept that your spouse may have a different money relationship than you do.
- Talk about how each of your money relationships may be affecting your children in both positive and negative ways; talk about whether you're sending mixed messages that might confuse your children.
- Explore the roots of your money behaviors. Use the genogram to find the family pattern that has helped shape your money relationships, and talk about specific incidents growing up that produced your current attitude about financial matters.
- Talk to each other about how changing behaviors might benefit your children; emphasize the positive future benefits rather than the negative problems in the past.

Action Plan

An action plan doesn't have to be elaborate, but it helps if you write down a few things that you will do differently. Be specific about what you want to change and when you want to change it.

Small, doable changes are best. It's unrealistic to expect that you can change your money personality overnight. Target a behavior that you believe is negative, and do something to change it (rather than eliminate it). If you and your spouse agree that you spend too much time bragging about your accumulated wealth in front of the kids, you may write that "This week I'm not going to talk about how much money I've made." Many times, small adjustments are all that are necessary.

Your action might also be adding a behavior. In our previous example, for instance, Leon could have shown his children that he valued charitable endeavors. He could have signed up for a volunteer program with them, or he could have discussed his own involvement in philanthropy with his children and invited them to participate with him.

A Balanced Personality

The odds are that not only is your money personality different from that of your partner's, but it's different from those of your friends and neighbors. Although there are only three dimensions of money relationships, there are infinite variations within these dimensions. In the use category, for instance, one person may be a miser and another a spendthrift. But there are many types of misers and spendthrifts. Jill may hoard every penny she makes; Jane is very frugal about some things but not others. Plus, Jill may be a rigorous manager of money, but Jane is very cavalier about management. On top of that, Jill may be very verbal about the need to save money, but Jane rarely talks about it. Or Jill might feel tremendous anxiety about her miserliness, but Jane accepts her behaviors.

Whatever your money personality might be, you shouldn't feel that this personality is "wrong" just because it's different. Everyone has money quirks and says or does things related to money that they shouldn't. It's not the money personality you need to change but the extreme parts of that personality and how they're manifested when your children are around.

You want to regulate your relationships with money so that you are in the middle range of each of the three dimensions. You want to neither overregulate nor underregulate. Balance is the key.

4

The Value of Values

Two of our friends and their teenage daughter, Louisa, throw an annual holiday party in which they spare no expense. Their house is beautifully decorated, and the food is superb. When you drive up to their house, you're met by a valet service. You get out of your car and hand an unwrapped gift to a man dressed as Santa Claus, who places the gift in a large cardboard box, and you notice many boxes filled with presents. The purpose of these unwrapped gifts is explained in the invitation:

> *Our family is blessed, that's true,*
> *so we would like to try something new.*
> *In lieu of pretty presents, glorious gifts, and sweets,*
> *we would like to spoil some special moms and kids*
> *with some very meaningful treats.*
> *A soft nightie, sweater, cozy slippers, or yummy shampoo,*
> *Anything to make her feel special will generously do.*
> *Warm clothes, videos, balls, or a stuffed toy*
> *would bring a smile to each special girl or boy.*
> *An unwrapped gift for a "Mom or Child in Mind"*
> *would be so appreciated and very kind.*
> *Thanks for helping us support*
> *a home for*
> *battered mothers and children . . .*

Here is the story of another party. A recent newspaper article reported that the average cost of a preschool party goody bag in a wealthy Los Angeles neighborhood exceeded $20. These bags—which used to hold inexpensive items like a plastic party horn and bubble gum—have become a source of competition among mothers. One mom was quoted in the article as saying, "Kids remember what they get and what they like, and if you're going to get in the game and compete, well, you have to be original. I know that sounds terrible, but you don't have a choice." Another mother, who spent $700 on goody bags for her son's fourth birthday party, said, "The kids would be happy with jelly beans, but this is the way I do things."

Consider how these two types of parties convey different money values. Louisa is learning the value of "enough"; she recognizes that she has enough and others do not through the charitable focus of the invitation and the participatory process of learning about the charity, collecting the gifts, and transporting them to people in need. Even though the party is lavish, it helps instill the value of sharing with people who are less privileged. On the other hand, some of the kids who host or go to these expensive goody-bag parties absorb the value of "too much." For them, excess becomes the norm; extravagance becomes acceptable behavior. It's not hard to imagine these little kids growing up and competing with friends and neighbors to see who can build the biggest house or buy the most luxurious car. Some of these kids won't give a moment's thought to sharing because they never feel as though they have enough.

It's entirely likely, however, that many of these Los Angeles parents don't realize the negative money values being conveyed. The majority of them probably have good bedrock values, and they would be aghast if they realized that they might be teaching their kids greed and selfishness. Some of them think expensive goody bags are "cute"; others believe that they're spending money on these treats out of love for their children and a desire to make them look good. Because of these adults' relationships with money, however, their decent values become distorted when communicated as money values.

Remember, affluence is a double-edged sword. In and of itself, a wealthy lifestyle does no harm to children. When this lifestyle is unaccompanied by well-thought-out values, however, it can be psychologically destructive. When discussing the stages of a child's development and money relationships, we stressed the importance of highly conscious behaviors—that you need to be aware of what messages you're sending to your children when you're dealing with money. Sometimes it's difficult to know what these messages are because so many of our interactions with children are not thoroughly thought out or analyzed. Most of us don't go around asking ourselves, "What message am I going to send to Janie if I say *X* versus saying *Y*?"

If we can clarify our general values, however, we are much more likely to pass on positive types of money values to our children. Rather than allow our own uneasy relationships with money to taint the values we pass on to our kids, we must be in touch with our sacred beliefs—our belief in honesty, truth, fairness, equality, and other life-affirming concepts—and make sure these beliefs are reflected by our money behaviors. To help clarify your money values, let's look at values from both general and parenting perspectives.

What Is a Value?

Sociologist Milton Rokeach suggests that a value represents a result you believe is important, not just now but in the long run.

Values help shape your behavior and help you deal with tough questions; they help you figure out the "right" thing to do and say in complicated situations. For instance, let's say you live in a community that has a view of beautiful, undeveloped, rolling foothills.

In fact, you bought your house because it afforded you a great view of the landscape. At the same time, you've always been dismayed by the homogeneity of your community. You wish it were more economically and racially diverse so your children could be exposed to different types of people. One day an announcement is made that a real estate developer plans to build low-cost housing in the foothills, the only parcel of land available in the community large enough for this type of development. Although the low-cost housing will make the community more diverse, it will also spoil your view and damage the fragile ecology of the foothills.

Deciding what to do in this situation is difficult. If you favor the development, you lose your view. If you're against the development, you're a hypocrite because of your long-held belief in diversity. Complicating matters, you can rationalize being against the development because you also are an environmentalist and believe it will harm the environment. Complicating things further, you worry about the crime and lowered property values that sometimes accompany low-cost housing. If you haven't clarified your values, you may not know what to do or, even worse, do something that contradicts your values.

Viktor Frankl, an Austrian neurologist and psychoanalyst, writes movingly about values. His autobiography, *Man's Search for Meaning* (which details his experiences in the Nazi death camps), communicates how his strong values helped him survive the concentration camps. He writes that the answer to life's challenges "must consist, not in talk and meditation, but in right action and in right conduct. Life ultimately means taking the responsibility to find the right answer to its problems and to fulfill the tasks which it constantly sets for each individual."

Frankl emphasizes that values should be the touchstones of our lives; when all else fails, they guide our actions. It's not only guidance that they provide, however, but values-based happiness. As both parents and counselors, we've found that people who live in accordance with their values enjoy happy lives. More relevantly, children who live in accordance with their values enjoy an identity; they are able to measure their accomplishments against it and answer the question, "What kind of person am I?" Thus, by passing on well-thought-out values to our children, we help them achieve values-based happiness and give them a moral compass with which to navigate their way for years to come.

Steven Reiss, a psychologist at Ohio State University, has identified and defined sixteen basic human desires that strike us as a good starting point for thinking about values. Though a list of possible values could go on for pages, these sixteen desires will help you start thinking about your values (what we desire is closely related to what we value) and which ones you embrace emotionally, intellectually, and behaviorally. Without value clarity, we can easily pass on the wrong or confusing values to our children by how we deal with money issues. Review the following list adapted from Reiss's work, and see which desires seem to apply to you:

Power—the desire to influence others
Independence—the desire for self-reliance
Curiosity—the desire for knowledge
Acceptance—the desire for inclusion
Order—the desire for organization
Saving—the desire to collect things
Honor—the desire to be loyal to one's parents and heritage
Idealism—the desire for social justice
Social Contract—the desire for companionship
Family—the desire to raise one's own children
Status—the desire for social standing
Vengeance—the desire to get even
Romance—the desire for sex and beauty
Eating—the desire to consume food
Physical activity—the desire for exercise
Tranquility—the desire for emotional calm

Children learn values from their parents, their teachers, their friends, the media, and from society. As they grow and enter school, they begin to test these values. By the time they are adults, they should have developed their own value systems. If our children received consistent messages about values from all of these sources, they could apply those values easily to every choice they face in daily life. Our children would be prepared to choose among conflicting alternatives, and their behavior would always be consistent with their values. The problem is that they must grapple with conflicting values: what we might be trying to teach our children about the importance of moderation is likely to be in conflict with the values they learn from friends, television commercials, popular magazines, or even the president of the United States. We cannot anticipate every situation that our children will encounter, but if we instill basic values in our children, we will have given them standards of right and wrong that they can apply in difficult situations. If our children do not have basic standards of right and wrong, they will be more likely to make decisions based on peer pressure and the power of the media. They will listen to friends and ads and respond, "Everybody in my class smokes pot; it can't be wrong." Or, "Cool people wear $350 Porsche Design sunglasses; I need a pair."

A wonderful story about making decisions based on values rather than peer pressure involves our youngest son, Kevin. When Kevin was growing up, we lived in the rather bohemian town of

SILVER NUGGET

Think about what your children value most. Does what they value correspond with your personal beliefs?

Venice, California, a few blocks from Alan's, a tiny, independent market. One day when he was five years old, Kevin and Eileen were grocery shopping, and Kevin asked for Cap'n Crunch cereal. Eileen said no; it had too much sugar. A few moments later she found Kevin with an open box of Cap'n Crunch and a mouth full of cereal. Eileen escorted Kevin to the front of the store, and Alan, seeing the open box of cereal and sensing what had happened, explained to Kevin that Eileen hadn't wanted to buy the cereal but now she had to pay for it and Kevin would have to figure out how to pay her back. Kevin did odd jobs around the house until the money was repaid. Eleven years later, Kevin had a part-time summer job as an usher at a local movie theater. He found an expensive portable CD player while cleaning up one evening and turned it in to the manager. He told us that the other ushers jeered and called him a dummy and a dork. We congratulated him on his honesty and asked him how he arrived at the decision to turn it in despite overwhelming peer pressure to keep it. His reply was, "The Cap'n Crunch incident taught me that it was wrong to take a box of cereal. How could I take an expensive CD player that belonged to someone else?"

Values aren't values unless they have emotional, intellectual, and behavioral components. In other words, we might believe intellectually and emotionally that honesty is important, but it's not a value if our behavior at work is dishonest. When it comes to the values we pass on to our children, this point is crucial. They need to know we care deeply about a value (emotional), that we think about it long and hard when considering choices and consequences (intellectual), and that we act in accordance with our values (behavioral).

Children will spot "value hypocrisy" faster than you might imagine. Nothing sends a more destructive message about values than a parent whose actions pay only lip service to values. You may lecture your children on the need to be polite and courteous to others, but what message do you send when you treat salespeople disdainfully at a department store? The last thing you want to do is confuse or disillusion your children about your values, especially when they're "expressed" in relation to money matters.

What Is a Money Value?

Money values are the way we translate day-to-day values into our relationship with money. They're communicated based on how we acquire, manage, and use money. Our behavior around money tells our children more about our money values than anything we say. Our children may accept our money values or they may reject them, but we guarantee you that they won't ignore them.

Whatever your values are, they can often become muddled when they are translated into money values. You may strongly believe in honesty, yet your child observes you talking on the phone and encouraging an employee to do something deceptive to save the company money on a deal. Or you may place a high value on humility yet spend in ways that your child believes you are "showing off." Or your constant fretting about every nickel spent may contradict your value of generosity. When you're conscious of your basic values, you can do a better job of making sure your money values are consistent.

Affluence can create a disconnection between our general values and our money values. Sometimes we develop a double standard and are able to believe one thing while we do another.

A well-to-do lifestyle can go to our heads, and we can start acting in ways that have little to do with who we are. Because we have it, we spend it, and our willingness to shower money on everyone—including our children—may be divorced from what we believe is important. Affluence may also make us arrogant with our money; we may brag about how much we have out of a misplaced sense of pride.

David Brooks describes this phenomenon in *Bobos in Paradise: The New Upper Class and How They Got There*. *Bobos* are *bo*urgeois *bo*hemians earning hundreds of thousands of dollars a year. Bobos have developed "a code of financial correctness" that allows them to spend lavishly on anything they are able to categorize as needs rather than mere wants. As Brooks observes, "You can spend as much as you want on anything that can be classified as a tool, such as a $65,000 Range Rover with plenty of storage space, but it would be vulgar to spend money on things that cannot be seen as tools, such as a $60,000 vintage Corvette." Brooks explains that "a person who follows these precepts can dispose of up to $4 million or $5 million annually in a manner that demonstrates how little he or she cares about material things."

Awareness of how you are translating your values into money values will keep you grounded and focused. It can make you aware of the distorted thinking that Brooks describes in *Bobos* and help you deal with difficult decisions, especially where your kids are concerned.

How Do We Clarify Our Money Values?

Before we can talk to our children about money, we need to have identified and clarified our money values. To understand how the process works, let's look at a couple we recently worked with.

Jerry is a successful entrepreneur. Susan is a pediatrician. They are in their late forties and have been married for five years. Each has adolescent children by prior marriages. Their home has been a merry-go-round, with the children living part-time with them and part-time with the other parents. Jerry is paying child support to his ex-wife, and Susan is receiving child support from her ex-husband. A few years ago, Jerry and Susan retained Jon to help plan their estates. During their first meeting, Jon explained that they should develop an estate plan that not only saved taxes but also incorporated their basic family money values. Jon said that doing so involved clarifying their money values and incorporating those values into a family mission statement that makes up the heart of the estate plan. In the corporate world, a mission statement communicates the essence of an organization to its shareholders, employees, and the public. A family mission statement goes beyond this by describing who you are, what you are doing with your life, and why you are doing it. In other words, you define what your values are, what you value, and what you are doing to achieve or reflect these values.

Susan, however, protested that they didn't have time to create a mission statement. They were leaving for Hawaii in two weeks on a family vacation and wanted a simple estate plan, "just in case anything happened on the trip." Jerry said they would consider Jon's suggestions when they returned.

Jon didn't hear from them again for several months when they asked to meet with the two of us. Jerry explained that they were facing a dilemma. Each of them had a sixteen-year-old by a prior marriage who was going through that most important of Southern California rites of passage: obtaining a driver's license. Both teenagers wanted new cars—Jerry's daughter wanted a BMW convertible, and Susan's son had his eye fixed on a Mazda Miata—and both expected Jerry and Susan to pay for them. Jerry's daughter had been told by her mother that Jerry had much more money than she did and that he should buy her a car. Susan's son said that his father told him that he had paid child support for years and that Susan should buy him his car.

Susan said that they found themselves facing some conflicting issues they were having trouble resolving:

- They had the money and could afford to buy new cars for the children.
- The idea of buying expensive new cars for sixteen-year-olds was ludicrous to them.
- Jerry didn't want to look cheap by comparison to the parents of other children at the school their kids attended, because many of them had bought cars for their sons and daughters.
- Both Jerry and Susan were bothered by their children's sense of entitlement.

They remembered Jon's comments last year about the need to clarify their money values and develop a family mission statement. They were curious how the process of value clarification worked and whether it would help them deal with their conflicts over whether to buy cars for their children.

We explained that most of what is known about value clarification stems from work done in the '60s by three psychologists, Louis Raths, Merrill Harmin, and Sidney Simon, who developed a three-stage process. They called the stages "Prizing," "Choosing," and "Acting." Other authors have adopted slightly different names. In their excellent book *What Matters Most*, Hyrum W. Smith and Ken Blanchard referred to these stages as "Discover," "Plan," and "Act."

No matter what we call them, the three stages translate into the following three actions:

1. Identifying what is important to us about money
2. Selecting among alternatives
3. Acting in a manner that is consistent with our money values

This process doesn't tell you what your money values ought to be. Rather, it's educational. It helps you identify and articulate your money values. Once you have identified your money values, you can decide whether those values are truly helpful or counter-productive in your life and need to be changed.

SILVER NUGGET

Think about a situation where you faced a value conflict involving your children; did you resolve the conflict by sticking to your values or by doing what your children wanted?

Stage One: Identifying What Is Important to Us

The first stage in clarifying money values is the prizing, or discovery, phase, where we gain insight by identifying and understanding how money is important to us. This phase involves identifying and understanding the role that money plays in our lives.

We told Jerry and Susan that we use four simple steps to help our clients through this first stage. Married couples complete the first three steps separately and then treat the fourth step as a joint project.

Step One: Make a list detailing how money is important to you. In identifying what money meant to her, Susan listed (1) security, (2) not worrying, (3) opportunities it presents for us and our children, (4) knowing we have enough, and (5) the ability to give to charity. Jerry's list included (1) security, (2) money as a scorecard and indicator of status, (3) acquisition as a game, (4) control over my environment, and (5) philanthropy.

Step Two: Make a list of what you want your children to learn about money. Interestingly, there is often a significant difference between what money may represent to you and what you might wish it to represent to your children. Jerry's list is a case in point, consisting of (1) not being afraid of money, (2) viewing money as a tool that is neither good nor bad, (3) learning that money is not a scorecard, (4) being philanthropic, and (5) managing money prudently. Susan's list included wanting her children to know (1) it's not the most important thing in life, (2) money is neither good nor bad—what one does with it is important, (3) how to manage it well, (4) how to live within their means, (5) how to use money wisely, (6) how they get money and how they spend it, and (7) how to give some of it away to charities.

Step Three: Complete the sentences. Jerry and Susan were then asked to use their respective lists as the basis for completing as many of the following sentences as possible. We reminded them that this step was not a collaborative effort; each needed to work alone. We also told them that they might find that some of the sentences were not applicable. If so, they should skip them. We also asked them to take as much time as they needed, whether it was a few minutes or a few days, to complete the sentences. We are listing their answers below each question.

- I learned that I . . .
    Susan: *"focused mostly on wanting my children to learn how to use money."*
    Jerry: *"have never really thought about the effect of my money values on my children."*
- I never realized before that I . . .
    Jerry: *"have money values that are quite different from the values I want my children to have when they grow up."*

- I was saddened to realize that I . . .
  Jerry: *"treat money as a scorecard even though I don't want my children to treat it that way."*
- I believe that money . . .
  Jerry: *"shouldn't form the basis on which I judge people."*
  Susan: *"presents us with challenging opportunities."*
- The best thing I ever bought was . . .
  Jerry: *"my home."*
  Susan: *"a trip to Europe when I was twenty-one."*
- The most difficult thing about being affluent is . . .
  Jerry: *"figuring out how much to spend on my children without spoiling them."*
  Susan: *"distinguishing between needs and wants so far as our children are concerned—when to give and when not to give."*
- The greatest thing about being affluent is . . .
  Susan: *"the feeling of being secure and not worrying about money."*
- If I had an extra million dollars, I would . . .
  Jerry: *"invest it."*
  Susan: *"pay off the mortgage and give the rest to my favorite charities."*
- One money value I'm struggling to establish is . . .
  Susan: *"managing it more efficiently."*
- With regard to money, one thing I want to start doing right now is . . .
  Jerry: *"try to stop using money as a scorecard."*
  Susan: *"keeping a closer look at where our discretionary income is going."*
- I'm proud of using money to . . .
  Jerry: *"help others."*
  Susan: *"help others and to pay for our children's education."*

- I save money for . . .
  Jerry: *"investing."*
  Susan: *"travel."*
- I object to spending money on . . .
  Jerry: *"overpriced luxuries."*
  Susan: *"a lot of luxuries."*

Step Four: Develop a money philosophy of life. Jerry and Susan accomplished the first three steps separately. Now we asked them to collaborate in developing a joint family money philosophy. This is the family money mission statement Jon referred to in his first meeting with Jerry and Susan. We told Jerry and Susan to exchange their lists and completed sentences from the first three steps and use them as the basis for a frank discussion of their respective money values and the role that money plays in their lives. We then asked them to use that discussion as the basis for writing a short description of the role the two of them would like money to play in their family's life. We explained that we weren't expecting the great American novel but rather a paragraph or so that reflected their joint values. The result:

We want our affluence to be an opportunity, an opportunity to help our family grow and develop and an opportunity to help others less fortunate. Within our own family we need to realize that we weren't born entitled to be affluent. Good luck, like being in the right place at the right time, has played as important a part as education and hard work. Outside of our family we need to realize that others less fortunate weren't predestined to be poor. Bad luck has played a role in their situation.

For our own family, we want to manage our affluence prudently. This doesn't mean becoming misers or spending our entire lifetimes thinking about our wealth. It does mean paying our bills in a timely manner, living the "good life" within our means, and saving for investments and retirement. To do this, money has to be viewed by the family as a tool, not as a goal. We need to demystify money, so that finances can be discussed at the dinner table in the same way as politics, sports, and other issues of interest to us. Outside our family, it means not only giving to charity, but realizing that affluence should mean that we have the time to give not only of our money, but also of our time.

Stage Two: Choosing Among Alternatives

Once Jerry and Susan finished creating their joint family money philosophy, it was time for them to turn to the second stage of clarifying money values: choosing among alternatives. Once we have identified our money values, how do we distinguish among them? In many cases we need to choose between values that are equally important in the abstract. Do we give money to our school or our church or synagogue? What's more important: spending money on a big family vacation or taking smaller, less-expensive vacations and putting the savings in a fund for the children's college education?

Stage two is an extremely important aspect of our children's money education. Many children often have difficulty realizing there are alternatives. They tend to view situations as presenting only one course of action, even though there are other and better alternatives they hadn't thought of. If we do not learn to consider alternatives as children, we tend to make the same mistakes as adults. Perhaps you have found yourself saying, "If only I had thought of that first!" Many children also have difficulty in distinguishing alternatives in terms of potential outcomes. They frequently make choices based on the immediate consequences without thinking about long-range consequences. If the child is trying to save money to buy a new toy, spending the money on candy provides immediate gratification but defeats the long-term goal.

We use something we call the Alternatives Grid to help our clients choose among competing money values. You can use the Alternatives Grid to help your children learn to make choices. We asked Jerry and Susan to review the lists of money values that they wanted to impart to their children and to identify those money values that were relevant to the children's requests for new cars. After looking at the values they wanted to impart to their children, Susan and Jerry decided that two of their values were involved: living within their means and managing their money prudently. We suggested that they create an Alternatives Grid consisting of four columns, labeled "Alternative," "I'll Try It," "I'll Consider It," and "No, Thanks." In the "Alternative" column, they were to list as many responses as they could think of to their children's requests for a BMW convertible and a Mazda Miata. It doesn't matter if some of the alternatives are harebrained. They should then list their names in one of the three columns to the right. "I'll Try It" means that Jerry or Susan is willing to implement that alternative without further discussion. "I'll Consider It" means that they are not willing to implement the alternative but would be willing to talk about it some more. Finally, "No, Thanks" means "over my dead body." The Alternatives Grid helps you decide what money behaviors are appropriate for your family. We told Jerry and Susan to be as specific as possible and suggested showing the Alternatives Grid to the children to illustrate the process of selecting alternatives. Pretty soon, the Alternatives Grid looked like this:

Alternatives Grid

Alternative	I'll Try It	I'll Consider It	No, Thanks
Buy them the cars; we can afford it.		Jerry	Susan
Buy them the cars; we don't want to look cheap to the other parents.			Susan and Jerry
Say no and get them nothing.			Susan and Jerry
Say no and get them cheaper cars.		Susan and Jerry	
Say no and give them enough money so they can either buy cheaper cars or save for more expensive cars.	Susan and Jerry		

The Alternatives Grid is an excellent tool when you are faced with a specific money value issue: should we make this purchase? Should we donate to this charity?

Stage Three: Acting

The final stage in values clarification is acting consistently with your money values. Based on the previous two stages, Jerry and Susan arrived at the following conclusions about what they should do. First, they felt that helping the children get cars was appropriate (a money value). Second, they decided that small cars were too dangerous for young drivers. Any first car would have to weigh at least 3,000 pounds and could not be a convertible (a general value). Third, they decided to give both children $15,000 that they could apply against the purchase price of a car that met their safety standards (another money value). They then met with the children and helped them identify several alternatives, including buying a used car for $15,000, asking their other parent to contribute, or getting a summer job and saving money for a more expensive car that would meet Jerry and Susan's safety standards.

Jerry and Susan were faced with a very specific money value issue: should they give their sixteen-year-old children cars? Some money value issues are more general and cannot be solved as easily. For example, you may be wondering if your overall lifestyle is consistent with your money values and whether it is sending the appropriate messages to your children. In these situations, two additional techniques are helpful: the Money Pie of Life and the Money Diary.

The Money Pie of Life.   The pie is a graphic rendition of your money behaviors. It is a powerful learning tool that helps you identify whether your money behavior is consistent with your money values. You can also use the Money Pie of Life with your children to help them evaluate their money values and money behaviors.

If you are already using a computer to balance your checkbook and pay your bills, print out a pie chart that organizes your expenditures last year by category. If not, go review last year's records and sort your expenditures into categories such as mortgage, insurance, cars, vacation, movies, and so on. Total up the categories, and draw a circle on a large piece of paper. It might look like the pie shown on page 78.

The Money Pie of Life shows where your money is going. Are you satisfied? Do you want to change the size of the slices, add new ones, or eliminate existing slices? What would be your ideal Money Pie? Consider how you could use the Money Pie of Life to help your ten-year-old understand where her allowance money is going and what alternatives she might have.

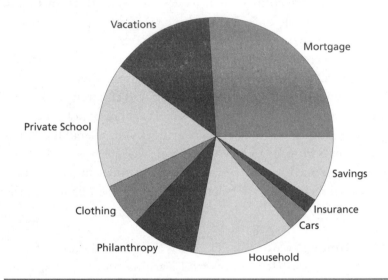

The Money Pie of Life.

The Money Diary. In Chapter 3 we shared part of a letter we had received from Alan and Marisa. In that letter, Marisa also mentioned:

We keep a notebook and record details of our spending or making money or stewardship of our possessions. We have a column for each category and then will add other thoughts or insights that come along.

The process allows me to really get out my emotional baggage from my conditioning (like the spend versus not-spend cycle). It allows me to share my ideas, and it's a safe place to air whatever I am dealing with financially. Because I'm trying to change, our meetings give me a place to look at what's happening and what we're doing, and then I can act on changing how I am and see that progress. The meetings give me a way to shape my own ideas about money instead of acting out of my conditioning.

Alan and Marisa were employing one of the most useful tools in value clarification: the Money Diary. This is another graphic means of understanding our money behaviors and determining whether they are congruent with our money values. The Money Diary is usually used for major purchases, although you can use it to track all of your expenditures. You have to decide on your definition of "major."

To create a Money Diary, take a piece of paper, create six columns, and label them as shown on page 80.

List each major purchase you make. Check whether you are glad or disappointed about the purchase. Indicate whether you made the purchase on your own or after speaking to others about their experiences with the same or similar products. In the sixth column, list the money values represented by the purchase. If you purchased the items on sale, a money value might be frugality. On the other hand, if you are disappointed because the item turns out to be shoddily made, the money value in question might be spending responsibly.

What have you learned about yourself and your relationship with money? How does money affect the way you live?

The Money Diary is a powerful family tool to use with your children, especially in conjunction with the Money Pie of Life. Combined, they become an ongoing family project used to track

The Money Diary

Purchase	Cost	Glad We Bought It	Disappointed We Bought It	Alone or with Others	Money Value

significant purchases, such as cars, computers, or vacation trips, and assess levels of satisfaction. They are also extremely useful techniques when talking with your children about their use of money.

As a final exercise, we'd like you to create a family money values continuum that will help your children identify their own relationships with money. In the last chapter, we discussed the three dimensions of your money relationships: acquisition, use, and management. We are going to reframe these adult relationships in terms that children can relate to.

Draw three parallel lines on a piece of paper. Label them as shown here:

Don't Need Much	Need A Lot

GET

Hoard	Spend It All

USE

Overly Concerned	Careless

TAKE CARE OF

Tell your children that you would like them to place themselves on each relationship line. Explain that the end of each relationship line represents a child who *always* feels or acts a particular way. Most children tend to feel or act more toward one end than toward the other, but they don't *always* feel or act that way. Tell them to put themselves in the middle only if they feel or act one way half the time and the other way the other half the time. If they feel or act more one way than the other, they should put themselves more toward that end. How close to the end they want to put themselves depends on how much of the time they feel or act that way.

Children get money in different ways. They may receive an allowance. They may obtain money gifts on holidays. They may be paid for chores around the house. Older children may have part-time jobs, such as a paper route or baby-sitting. In your family, they may have trust funds.

At one end of the "get" spectrum is the child who *always* feels that she doesn't need much money. At the other end of the relationship spectrum is the child who *always* feels that he needs a lot of money.

Children use money in different ways. At one end of this spectrum is the child who *always* puts all of his money in the piggy bank, or maybe Wells Fargo. At the other end is the child who spends it as soon as he gets it.

Children take care of money in different ways. At one end of this spectrum is the child who invariably misplaces his money or can never explain how he spent the money. The other end of the spectrum is the child who keeps track of every penny.

This exercise will help your children start identifying their money relationships at an early age and begin thinking about how their values impact each relationship dimension.

SILVER NUGGET

Next time your child receives what you consider to be a substantial sum of money as a gift, pay attention to how she uses it and takes care of it.

Time Well Spent

We've included many tools and techniques here to help you identify your money values. For some of you, it may seem like too much. You may already have done a good job defining your general values and understanding how they are translated into money values. It's possible that you can do a good job identifying your money values using some, but not all, of the steps and stages. We've found, however, that many of our clients and friends aren't clear about these issues. As we've emphasized, affluent people sometimes don't see how their money behaviors stand in direct contradiction to their bedrock values. Remember, money has a strong psychological undercurrent. Our actions may correspond with our values in other areas of our lives, but when it comes to use, acquisition, and management of money, we find ourselves out of sync with those values. Being aware that you're out of sync and taking steps to get back in sync is crucial, and the more value identification and adjustment tools you have at your disposal, the better. You'll also find these tools useful when you talk to your children about money, the subject of the next chapter.

5

Talking with Your Kids About Money

When it comes to kids and money, you have to watch what you say.

Clearly, the impact of your words is linked to the particular developmental stage your child is going through. Similarly, your own relationship with money, in terms of acquisition, use, and management, unconsciously shapes your words. A parent with a strong use pattern will talk to her child differently than someone who has an acquisition mind-set. Clarifying your values when it comes to money issues can also have a profound influence on what you say; learning to have value-consistent money conversations is something that doesn't come naturally to all parents.

At the same time, you don't need to walk around reviewing a list of developmental stages, money relationships, and values before sitting down and talking with your child. All we're suggesting is that you consider these issues as well as the impact your words can have given these three areas. As you'll discover here, maintaining this awareness will help you have better conversations with your child—better in the sense that you'll increase the odds of your child receiving an appropriate money message.

Our goal in this chapter is to help you communicate openly and honestly with your kids about money now so that they won't experience many problems—financial or emotional—later. To that end, let's look at what happens when parents attempt to talk to their kids about everything from philanthropy to snobbery.

A Loaded Subject: Why You Can't Talk About Money Without Talking About Other Things

For most parents, talking about money is difficult. More than one person has told us it was easier to talk to their kids about the facts of life than the facts of their finances. In her book, *Your Money, Your Self*, Arlene Modica Matthews says that we avoid talking about money for a number of reasons:

- The rules of etiquette tend to be modeled on the behavior of the very rich. Because the very rich have historically tended not to discuss money, talking about money became something that isn't done in "polite society."
- There is the superstition that talking about money is bad luck.
- Because we associate money with filth, avoiding the subject enables us to avoid feelings of shame. (Oh, you say, who associates money with filth? Matthews suggests that we think of the derivation of such common expressions as "stinking rich," making a "pot" of "filthy lucre" and "wallowing in money.")
- Because we associate money with self-esteem and self-image, not discussing the subject enables us to avoid being self-conscious.

Whether or not you agree with Matthews, you may well have found yourself reluctant to talk about money matters with your kids. But no matter how uncomfortable the thought of these conversations may make you feel, recognize the negative impact on your children if you don't have them. Giving money the silent treatment not only robs your kids of the skills needed to manage it, but it can also result in emotionally unhealthy attitudes toward it.

Some years ago, we conducted a survey of estate planners who worked with affluent parents whose children had reached adolescence or young adulthood and were immature, irresponsible, and unmotivated. One estate planner responded to our survey by writing, "[I say] to my clients whose children are disappointments, lazy, and fail to live up to their potential: no device that I can draft will make up for lessons that weren't learned as a child."

Silence, however, is not the only sin parents can commit in this regard. Some parents have little difficulty talking to their children about money, but they confuse talking about money with lecturing about money. It's all too easy to start a money conversation and end up with a lecture that incorporates the following: "Money doesn't grow on trees"; "Do you think I'm made of money?"; "Why, when I was your age, I had to walk ten miles every day . . ." You may be tempted to deliver your lessons about money like a teacher in a classroom. Lecturing your kids accomplishes just as much as when your parents lectured you; your kids tune you out as fast as you tuned out your parents! Because kids are brilliant at tuning out lectures, we need to focus on real conversations rather than well-intentioned but useless sermons.

Keep in mind, too, that whether or not you're aware of it, you're sending your kids money messages all the time. Through your actions and body language, you model attitudes that affect the type of money values your kids will develop. Overspending, penny-pinching, neurotic budget balancing, obsessive money-making schemes, and the like are all behaviors that affect a child's values. Therefore, don't think for a second that you do no harm by avoiding the topic.

You may, however, be the type of parent who is convinced that money conversations with your children will be a breeze. If so, see if you have difficulty with any of the following questions:

- Would you have a problem telling your children how much money you and your spouse make as well as your net worth?
- Do you mind if your children tell their friends and their friends' parents how much money you have?
- Do you know what to say when your child asks you to buy him something because "I know you can afford it"?
- When your child tells you that all her friends' parents have bought them _____ (fill in the blank with the latest craze), what will you say when she asks you for one?
- What would you do if you overheard your child telling his friend, "My parents make a lot more money than your parents, so you have to do what I want to do"?
- How will you explain to your child that she shouldn't consider herself better than others just because you live in a prosperous community?
- If your child will inherit a sizable sum of money or receive a large sum from a trust, what will you say and do to make certain that the money is not a disincentive to responsible behavior?
- If your child sees you fighting with your spouse about money, what will you say to your child about the money issues involved?
- What will you say to your child after he asks you to buy him a toy that you don't approve of?
- How do you explain to your child that money can't buy happiness when it seems to her you spend most of your time happily making money?

If you're like most parents, you will react with concern and confusion to at least some of these questions. You may have grown up in a household where money was a taboo topic, and it's difficult for you to broach the subject with your own children. Or it may be that you believe it's gauche to talk about the specifics of money; you feel it's fine to just inform your children that "we're comfortable" and leave it at that. Or you may worry that you and your spouse have very different ideas about how to talk to your kids about money and are sending them mixed messages.

SILVER NUGGET

What is the main memory you have of your parents (or just one of them) talking with you about money? Think about how it affected your own attitude about money.

What and how you communicate to a child about money determines not just if he's fiscally responsible but socially responsible as well. Parents who learn to talk about money in appropriate ways usually raise well-adjusted, responsible, and value-conscious kids.

The Ten Worst Things You Can Say

Before looking at the things you should be saying and the messages you should be communicating, let's consider the words that shouldn't leave your mouth. We've found that focusing on these no-no's can make people more conscious about their money talk and help them edit out certain types of messages that can have a negative impact. Without further ado, here are the ten worst things parents can say when talking to children about money.

1. **We can't afford it.** This leads our list because it's such a common, dishonest response to a child's request (obviously, if you really can't afford it, then the response is appropriate). Your child has asked you to purchase something and you don't want to. Maybe it's a $79 plastic action figure that you don't want to buy because you consider it overpriced junk, or maybe it's a $275 pair of aviator sunglasses that you consider to be too expensive for a twelve-year-old who has lost his last two pairs of $8 sunglasses. Maybe it isn't overpriced or inappropriate but simply the third thing your kid has asked you to buy him today, and you feel that enough is enough. As a parent, you need to be able to say no based on your values or your budget. State your values simply and in a manner that shows how those values relate to the topic at hand. "No, I've already bought you two things today that you wanted and that's enough." "Let's buy X running shoes because they pay their employees a living wage. I don't want to buy shoes from Y company because they use child labor." Saying you "can't afford it" is the easy way out. It's also dishonest; it involves lying to your child rather than explaining your values. It may instill a false impression of the family's actual financial situation, making your child needlessly anxious. And your child will probably see you buying other things, exposing the lie for what it is.

2. **We'll talk about it later.** This is fine to say if you follow through and talk about the money subject later. Many times, however, parents use this delaying tactic to avoid troubling money issues. This tactic, especially when it's repeated over time and forms a pattern, communicates to children that certain subjects can't or shouldn't be discussed. "Why were you and Mom fighting about how much it costs to send me to that summer camp?" is the type of question that might earn the "We'll talk about it later" response. Rather than using the question as a springboard for discussion of important issues—what is the fair cost for a service,

how do you measure the benefit versus the cost—parents end up demonstrating that these issues aren't worth talking about. Obviously, it takes more than one instance of this response to send this message, but when it becomes a patterned response, kids recognize what's happening. Plus, children see that you're being dishonest after this pattern is established; they know you have no intention of talking about it later. Thus, you send a doubly negative message.

3. **We'll pay you $100 for every A on your report card.** Variations on this gambit include "We'll increase your allowance if you clean your room" or "We'll get you that car you want if you can avoid getting a detention this semester." Bribery is not a particularly healthy child-raising policy. You are teaching your kids to associate being loved and getting paid with achieving goals, rather than achieving those goals to attain a sense of self-satisfaction. As your kid grows older, he is likely to associate using money to buy friends or love. And if your kid doesn't get As or avoid detentions, the failure to earn the money will be equated in his mind with failing to "earn" your love.

4. **Money is the root of all evil.** Woe be unto the parent who employs this adage. The Bible actually says that greed—the love of money—is the root of all evil. From our perspective, what's evil is hurting others in the quest to make money or being so obsessive about making money that it, rather than family and friends, becomes the top priority. If you communicate that money is evil, your children may well rebel and believe money is to be worshipped. Even if they develop a dislike of material things, they may also burden themselves with an inability to manage money. Kids who have been victimized by money-is-evil propaganda tend to disdain learning basic money-management techniques and can easily get themselves into chaotic financial situations.

5. **Time is money.** Time isn't money. Time is time. If you're always in a hurry and impressing your child with the importance of not wasting a minute, you're teaching her to place a monetary value on everything. We've seen parents try to impress their children with their hourly wages or go beyond the old adage when reprimanding their children for wasting time: "When you're an adult, you're not going to be allowed to dillydally around at work the way you do with your homework." Telling a child that you can't go to her dance recital because "someone in this family has to pay the bills" sends all sorts of negative messages about what's important in life.

6. **That's not an appropriate question.** If you want to make your child feel guilty about being a member of an affluent family, this response does the trick. Younger children, especially, ask questions like "Are we rich?" "How much money do you make?" and "Do we have more money than Aunt Susie?" When kids ask these questions, their underlying concern is "Am I secure?" and "Are you going to be able to take care of me?" Although you may feel that your kids are asking embarrassing questions, they're only embarrassing to adults who have developed a certain type of relationship with money.

In addition, if you treat your child's question as appropriate and decide to answer, don't preface your remarks with "This might not make sense now, but you'll understand when you're an adult." No matter how valuable your words may be, you've negated the effect by insulting their money intelligence. You need to talk about money issues as they affect their world. Younger children may not grasp the concept of being spoiled; they will understand it if you talk about how Jimmy's parents give him everything he wants, which is one reason he always grabs other kids' toys and screams, "Mine!"

7. **They're disgustingly rich.** This sentiment can come out many different ways in conversations with your child. You might make a disparaging comment about neighbors who flaunt their wealth, or you might make a negative remark about the thirty-year-old dot-com billionaire featured on the news. The net effect is to associate wealth with negative images in your child's mind. She may not differentiate good ways of being affluent from bad. To her, you're tarring all affluent people with the same brush. If you don't have many money discussions with your child, this may be the main source of her ideas about affluence. Unless you want your child to become an antimaterialistic ascetic, don't disparage wealthy people because they possess billions, because they are young and rich, or because they like to spend their money on expensive cars, boats, and homes.

8. **Don't ever let anyone know how much money we have.** Privacy is important. On the other hand, excessive secrecy breeds paranoia and distrust. Although you probably don't want your children discussing the details of your net worth with their friends, you also don't want them to view the family's finances as top secret. Money paranoia as a child can lead to unhealthy money relationships as an adult. We know of individuals who have been trained so well not to talk about money that they are unwilling to reveal their net worth to their financial advisors! A child who is taught to keep money details totally secret from everyone may find it difficult to have a trusting relationship with a spouse on any level, especially with finances. Keep a sense of balance. Stress the need for privacy without instilling distrust of others. Simply point out to your children that certain issues, including the family's finances, should stay within the family.

9. **Why don't you have your friends come over here; we have a _____, after all.** You can fill in the blank with *swimming*

pool, tennis court, or any number of expensive toys that might be attractive to kids. Even suggesting to a child that his friendships are based on the family's affluence is a terrible idea. You can foster cynicism in a child, who comes to believe that his friends only like him for what he has, rather than who he is. There are parents who are blatant about this issue, telling their children that they're going to buy a pool table or elaborate video-game setup because it will help them make friends. It's fine to buy these toys, but it's not a good idea to talk about them within the context of your child's friendships.

10. **Be thankful you don't live** *there.* The "there" might be everything from a poor urban neighborhood to a middle-class suburb. The implication is that life must be miserable for everyone who doesn't live in a community like your own. Although it may be appropriate to talk to your child about the problems in high-crime areas of the inner city or a homeless person living in a cardboard box under a freeway overpass, you need to be cautious about associating happiness with affluence. Kids should understand that money can't buy love or happiness. Fostering this false linkage between affluence and happiness can cause kids to pursue wealth as a means to a full, happy life. If they are successful in achieving wealth, they don't understand why they're not happy when they have all the things money can buy.

Variations on this statement can include everything from "If I had his money, I wouldn't have a care in the world" to "You don't know how easy your life is because of what we have." The former, envious statement communicates the power of money to solve all problems; the latter tells kids that their problems are rendered trivial by your affluence and that they have no right to feel anxious, depressed, fearful, and so on. They need to understand that affluence is emotionally neutral and that you can be happy or miserable no matter how much money you have.

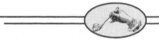

SILVER NUGGET

C hoose which of the ten worst things you're most likely to say and begin each day resolving not to talk to your child "in that way" about money.

Communicating an Abstract Concept

In one sense, it's easier to know what not to say than to figure out what to say and how to say it. If you've ever tried to have a serious talk with a small child about what money represents or with an adolescent about spending habits, you'll know that these conversations can be a challenge. When your small child becomes bored and starts to fidget or when your teenager's eyes glaze over, you've lost them. Abstract concepts can be tough for you to communicate and for kids to absorb, and financial subjects and the values that go with them can be very abstract.

Psychologists have developed a number of simple tests that allow you to see how small children handle money abstractions. Here are three you can try at home with your three- or four-year-olds:

• Make two rows of five pennies each. In the top row, put very little space between each one. In the bottom row, increase the space. The two rows ought to look like this:

○○○○○

○　○　○　○　○

Ask your child which row has more money in it. Most children choose the bottom row because it looks bigger.

• Put a dime and a nickel on the table and ask your child to pick the coin she wants. She will probably have no concept of the relative value of money and will pick the nickel because it's bigger.

• Put a dime in one hand and two nickels in the other and ask your child to choose. Once again, she'll probably choose the two nickels. Why? Because they look bigger and there are more of them.

Until a child is twenty-four to thirty months old, he isn't able to start stringing ideas together in a logical fashion. Suppose your two-year-old sees the dog in the backyard and says he wants to go outside. If you ask why, he'll most likely give you a blank look and a repetition of "Want to go out." Starting at about thirty months, he'll begin to develop the cognitive ability to connect ideas together in a logical manner and begin to understand the concepts of *why* and *because*. In fact, *why* and *because* quickly become kids' favorite comments! Asked the same question about going out, most four-year-olds can respond with a reason: "Because I want to play with the dog."

If we want to teach money values to our kids, we need to create an emotional and intellectual climate that helps them learn to think logically and to deal with abstract concepts. In their books *Building Healthy Minds* (by Stanley Greenspan) and *The Irreducible Needs of Children* (by Greenspan and T. Berry Brazelton), Greenspan and Brazelton, two of the United States' most renowned experts in child development, tell us that the keys to our children's learning to deal with such abstract concepts as money are a combination of reflective dialogue and floor time.

In a reflective discussion, you don't simply respond "yes" or "no" to your child's questions or comments. Instead, you ask what, when, why, and how to help them form an opinion and reflect on their own wishes and ideas, the foundation of abstract thinking.

Floor time is nothing more than setting aside at least twenty to thirty minutes of uninterrupted time every day to get down on the floor with your child. If both parents work, there is still plenty of room for floor time. Turn off the TV and turn on the answering machine. Being at your kid's level, eye to eye, generates a sense of equality. Floor time is a time when your kid owns you. During floor time, do whatever your child wants to do, even if it means playing the same game for the zillionth time. There should be no rules except no hurting people and no breaking toys. Let your child set the emotional tone of the play and follow his lead. As you talk and play and interact, you are establishing an environment in which your child feels comfortable in talking about anything.

In *Building Healthy Minds*, Greenspan reports that a study he carried out with Arnold Sameroff, of the University of Michigan, showed that children whose parents consistently used reflective discussions during floor time starting at thirty months were twenty times more likely to have normal to superior intelligence! Greenspan and Brazelton's most recent book, *The Irreducible Needs of Children*, talks about hanging-out time. This is simply floor time spent with older kids. You don't need to be on the floor with your teenagers, but they continue to need your undivided attention, and you need to leave your agenda behind.

Whether it's floor time or hanging-out time, by not having an agenda, you are allowing your child's agenda to emerge. In such an environment, children feel free to speak about what is on their minds. Money or money matters will inevitably come up. If your kid talks about a new toy or a pair of fancy sunglasses he bought, you can ask, "How do you feel about it? Is it worth it?" in a non-judgmental way. In the middle of play, your eight-year-old might suddenly say, "I wish I had $1 million." An appropriate response might be, "Well, if you had $1 million, what would you do?" In this way, you are able to explore how your child thinks and give him an opportunity to explore your mind. In his book *The Developing Mind*, neurologist and psychiatrist Daniel J. Siegel observed that this type of conversation leads your child to "feeling felt" and enhances secure attachment.

Floor time offers you the ability to share your beliefs, ideas, and intentions. Kids—especially younger children—love and understand entertaining stories that make a point. If they're asking what it's like to be poor, and you grew up in a less-affluent household than the one you are in now, tell them about your experiences. Or you can use a "money hero," or "money model," to illustrate a concept. Money heroes are people who have used money in a way that you find to be admirable, and their stories are ones your kids should hear about. Here is a sampling of stories about these money heroes:

• In the late 1800s, Mary Choate and a number of upper-class women formed the Women's Exchange, a chain of nonprofit retail stores that devoted their profits to widows and poor women. The chain became so popular that it competed with some of the giant retailers of the day.

• Edgar Helms, a Boston Methodist minister at Morgan Memorial Chapel, created Morgan Memorial Cooperative Industries and Stores in 1905. He had the idea of having volunteers go door-to-door to collect used clothing, shoes, and furniture. Helms would train and pay people who were out of work or disabled to restore the items and sell them at Morgan Memorial Stores. Within a year, 1,150 people were on the payroll. Today, Morgan Memorial Cooperative Industries and Stores is known as Goodwill Industries, one of the largest nonprofit organizations in America.

• In 1982 Paul Newman created a company that would sell salad dressing to local stores and give the money to charity. Today, Newman's Own is a multinational corporation that has given more than $100 million to charity.

• David Sun and John Tu founded Kingston Technology, the world's leading independent supplier of memory modules for personal computers. When they sold the company for $2 billion, they gave several hundred million dollars away to their employees to thank them for their hard work. Every employee got a bonus; the lowest was $75,000!

• Ken Voigt runs a used-car dealership in Ohio. In 2000 he came up with the idea of asking people to donate their used cars, whether or not they ran. Voigt fixes up the cars, sells them at a discount to people in the community who couldn't otherwise afford a car, and gives 85 percent of the net proceeds to Our Lady of the Wayside in Avon, Ohio, a home for mentally and physically challenged adults.

Don't feel limited by this handful of stories. The odds are you know a few of your own, stories about friends or relatives who used their affluence for the common good. It's also relatively easy to do research on the Internet at any one of a number of Good Samaritan sites and learn about the philanthropic efforts of individuals. Or, if you're creative, you may be able to create your own fable that will illustrate how individuals can use money for selfless, rather than selfish, ends. Although stories don't always work—simple, clear answers to questions are equally important—they often are more memorable than a statement of fact. Both types of communication tools, however, can help you make the abstract concept of money more accessible for your child.

Teachable Times: Being Alert for the Moment When Money Messages Can Be Sent

In the real world, you can be staggeringly eloquent about fiscal responsibility and tell spellbinding stories of money heroes, and your child may not hear a word you say. As much as you may want to talk about money issues, your children may not be prepared to listen. As a result, parents must be alert for those moments when their kids are open-eared and open-minded when it comes to financial subjects. As we noted earlier, if you let them lead the discussion during floor time, they may well broach this subject themselves.

Smaller children especially are curious about everything, including money. Think back to when you were growing up. Did you wonder how much money your parents had, what your house cost, and how much your father or mother made each year? Your curiosity caused you to articulate these questions, and when you did, you created a teachable moment. This is your window to communicate the information and the values you want to impart to your child.

Although there are many teachable moments, the following list of such moments will help you be aware of some of the more common ones:

- Your child is toddling around the house, picks up a coin on the floor, and asks, "What's this?"
- You're at a store (often a toy store or grocery store), and your child points at something and asks, "How much does this cost?"
- You and your spouse are debating a money issue, and your child asks what you're talking about.
- Your child asks you if you're rich.
- Your child's friend receives an expensive gift, your child wants the same thing, and you want to say "no" because you consider it too expensive or inappropriate.
- You tell your child she is going to receive an allowance (or your child asks for a raise in that allowance).
- You drive through a dilapidated neighborhood, and your child asks, "Are these people poor?"

- You open a checking account for your child, or give him a few shares of stock (or some other investment vehicle).
- Your child asks for something relatively expensive, and you explain that he has to earn it.
- You lose your job or make some other major life change and have to or want to downshift your lifestyle as a result.
- Your child asks what he can do to help those less fortunate than himself.
- You pass someone on the street asking for a handout.

You can also create teachable moments on your own. For instance, if you are taking the family to Disney World, let the teenagers help figure out the budget. Younger children might lack the skills for budgeting, but they can be given the opportunity to help make decisions after the budget is completed. Give them a fixed dollar amount to spend during the day, and don't bail them out if they lack sufficient funds for one more soft drink or ride.

Expect your child to make mistakes, and recognize that these mistakes provide prime teachable moments. For instance, we had taken our twelve-year-old son with us to San Francisco and were staying in one of the city's finest hotels. We had given him permission to order breakfast from room service. When we were checking out and received the bill, we noticed an $18 laundry charge. Because we hadn't sent anything out to be cleaned, we asked our son if he had done so. He explained his T-shirts were dirty and he had decided the hotel service could wash them. We made it clear to him that this wasn't acceptable; ordering meals from room service was OK, but it wasn't financially prudent to have $10 worth of T-shirts cleaned for $18. He understood that we weren't upset about the money but about the waste of money on an unnecessary extravagance. Because we dealt with the problem immediately and when he was most receptive to what we had to say, it helped him to learn to distinguish between reasonable and unreasonable spending.

Age Differences

You obviously need to talk about money differently with your children depending on their ages. We find it convenient to think in terms of four age ranges: under age five, from six to twelve, from thirteen to eighteen, and young adult. These are fairly loose groupings and where your child fits depends on his or her sophistication. Let's look at the first three of these groups. (We'll deal with young adults in Chapter 10 because their issues are significantly different and more complex than the others.)

Ages Five and Under

Until children are two or so, money has absolutely no meaning. Your children, however, are sensitive to your moods and can pick up on the fact that you are anxious or calm in different situations. The issue here isn't so much what you say to your kids about money but what you communicate through your tone of voice, body language, and interactions with your spouse. A three-year-old may not associate paying bills with money, but he will remember if your financial attitude about paying bills involves anxiety and controversy between you and your spouse. As he gets older, he will begin to associate those emotions with money.

Although you can't have a heart-to-heart money talk with your four-year-old, you can communicate with him indirectly. Think about establishing a consistent, middle-of-the-road emotional stance when it comes to your money behaviors around your small child. If you're going around the house clutching bills in your hand and raging against the utilities or if you're constantly bickering with your spouse about his spending habits, you are "saying" all the wrong things to your child.

Another way you communicate with your child is through the television programs you allow her to watch. Much has been written about the negative impact of television on young minds, but our take on the subject is a bit different. We strongly believe that you should limit your preschool child's exposure to television advertising because of her natural "wanting" tendency. Infants want to be fed and changed; they want adults with whom they can form a secure attachment. All of us talk to our babies and ask them if they want to eat, to take a nap, or to play. Advertising, however, can help push this wanting from normal to abnormal levels. The slickness and sophistication of many television commercials can create a sensory environment where children are virtually programmed to want things. Even if they can't understand the precise significance of a commercial, they can easily sense that a soft drink, a car, or a computer game is highly desirable. An environment that stimulates a young child's wanting impulse is especially dangerous in affluent homes, where wants can be easily translated into needs and needs into purchases.

What preschoolers can and should learn, however, is the concept of saving. In *Building Healthy Minds*, Greenspan suggests that, around age three, kids start to develop the ability to think logically and begin to connect concepts. They make these connections in a very literal manner, as we saw in the experiment in which a young child selects a nickel rather than a dime because the nickel is larger. We can take advantage of that literalness to teach preschoolers the concept of saving. Our friends Mark and Christie have a three-year-old daughter, Gail. When Mark gets home from work every evening, he empties his pants pockets of change and gives the coins to Gail. Instead of using a traditional piggy bank, Gail puts the change in a clear glass jar. Although she doesn't know the difference between pennies and dimes, she sees the jar filling up and relishes the notion of accumulating quantities of coins. Gail is also beginning to make the connection between giving money and getting something back in return, a concept that most preschoolers can grasp. Mark and Christie are helping their daughter learn this concept by having Gail put the change in the parking meter. She is beginning to understand that you need to give something (money) in exchange for something else (a place to park).

In another year or two Gail will probably recognize the difference between wants and needs. Understanding this difference is vital. It helps children learn to make choices among alternatives and avoids creating a sense of entitlement. To the entitled child, everything she wants is a need. Numerous opportunities arise during the average day to help a child learn the difference between wants and needs. For example, if you are going out for an ice cream cone after dinner, you can discuss the difference between needing to eat dinner and wanting to have an ice cream cone. You can make it a game by having the child classify things she sees as wants or needs. You might see a mother carrying an infant and ask whether the infant wants to have a caregiver or needs one.

Six to Twelve Years Old

Although it's fine to loosen up restrictions on watching television commercials at this point—school-age kids are less susceptible to the wanting impulse than preschool children—parents still need to set limits. Moderation in the time spent in front of the television is a good policy at this and other ages. Perhaps the most significant issue for this age group is buying things. This is the point when kids start making purchases on their own, and parents need to exercise a guiding influence. Watch your child's favorite television program with her and use it as an opportunity to talk about the money values illustrated by the program and the commercials.

As part of this influence, parents can provide children with an allowance, the subject of the next chapter. For now, you should understand that it's good to start kids on allowances earlier rather than later. Most younger children in this age category are prone to immediate gratification and are likely to blow their allowances on whatever strikes their fancy, regretting later that they no longer have any money to buy what they really want. If you wait to give your child an allowance until he's about age eleven, you'll find that he will encounter budgeting problems with his allowance that can lead to fierce arguments with you. It's better if you start the allowance process earlier and let kids make their budgeting mistakes when they're less likely to engage you in emotional battles over their insufficient funds. Younger children can and should make learning mistakes so that when they're older, they'll be better able to handle their allowances. Kids as young as age eight can be taught to budget and select from among alternatives if you will take the time to explain the process. After a few mistakes, children this age usually get it that they have to choose between *A* and *B* based on which one is more important to them. When you talk to your children about money, talk in terms of choices and their consequences.

It's also a great idea to revolve a conversation around opening a savings account at the local bank. When your child is around age eight, go with her to the bank, help her fill out the forms and then talk about what you've just done—with "props" in hand (checkbook, statements, calculator, etc.). This is an opportunity for you and your child to talk about checks and cash gifts she will be receiving for birthdays, Hanukkah, or Christmas. Discuss whether a portion of each gift should be put in the savings account. If philanthropy is a strong element of your money values, talk about whether a portion of each gift should go into a separate account that will be given to charity each year. Here are some other great questions that can be part of the conversation:

- What is the purpose of the savings account?
- What is the money being saved for?
- When can she withdraw the money?

- Can she spend the money in the savings account without your permission?

Finally, you'll find children in this age group will become aware of lifestyle differences between your family and others (friends, relatives, people in movies and on television shows, etc.). They will be naturally curious about why a neighbor has three cars and you only have two. They'll wonder why your house is so much larger and more luxurious than cousin Billy's. They'll start questioning you about a story they read that profiled a poor family and how they barely had enough to eat; they'll want to know why you can't give that family enough food so they don't have to be hungry anymore. Capitalize on these opportunities to discuss your values and to explain how those values are reflected in the way your family makes choices on how you spend money.

Thirteen to Eighteen Years Old

Money, not to mention affluence, carries with it responsibility, and adolescence is the time to expand learning to be responsible for how you spend and save your money. When you talk to your kids about money, address issues such as the cost of a given item versus its value to the individual, what constitutes an "overpriced" product or service, and the idea of setting and adhering to a reasonable budget. What may seem like simple issues to you are often mystifying for teenagers. Kids who have grown up in an affluent environment sometimes lack any sense of fiscal responsibility and are lost when it comes to making buying choices within a budget. Helping your child learn to master this type of responsible spending carries larger lessons about living one's life in an accountable, thoughtful manner.

You can do a number of things to foster discussions with your teenager about money, including having him open a checking account where he can deposit his allowance as well as gifts that aren't earmarked for a savings account. Keeping the checking account in balance is great training in budgeting and money management. A credit card should be viewed in the same light. The card should have a limit rationally related to the child's allowance and ability to pay. Giving a teenager an unrestricted credit card simply teaches him to spend. Many credit card issuers have a minimum limit of $1,000. In such a case, you and your teenager need to agree on a self-imposed lower limit. If that limit is reached or exceeded, the card needs to be put away until it is paid down below the limit.

Ideally, your thirteen-year-old already will have learned to allocate her allowance among fixed expenses, weekly personal spending, and savings. As allowances increase and as additional money comes in through part-time jobs, budgeting tasks and spending choices become more complex. In addition, your teenager should be encouraged to budget for longer periods of time than she did when she was younger—have her create a budget for the entire month or even a school quarter or semester. Talk about the budget, both before she creates it and afterward if she finds it's not right. When kids are shocked to discover their budgets were ill-conceived (especially when they were confident that they had created a perfect budget), they're open to learning and correcting their mistakes.

Sara's first try at creating a monthly budget was an eye opener for her. She had been receiving $10 a week allowance and had recently started earning an extra $10 on Saturday mornings by baby-sitting for a neighbor who was taking a yoga class. When she turned fourteen, her parents decided to change her allowance to $50 a month and give her the entire amount at the start of the month. Sara was encouraged to create a monthly budget. She assumed that she would have $90 a month. Her budget provided for her to put $20 of her allowance into her savings account at the start of each month and have available to spend the remaining $30 of her allowance as well as the $40 she would earn baby-sitting. The budget crashed in the first week. Sara spent the remaining $30 of her allowance on a pair of "absolutely fabulous" leather pants on sale at the local mall, and her next-door neighbor sprained her ankle and dropped out of the yoga class. After a discussion, Sara and her parents decided to go back to a weekly allowance for the next six months. Sara also realized that she needed to find other baby-sitting opportunities during the month.

You should also attempt to involve your children in researching major purchases. If you are going to purchase a new car or replace the refrigerator, let teenagers get on the Internet and help you evaluate both product quality and price. Such participation not only makes them responsible in part for the purchase, but offers you the chance to talk about money issues in a way that directly involves them.

Translating Appropriate Values into Words

One of the most difficult challenges for parents is communicating positive values in the heat of money conversations. When your child asks you a confusing question or pushes your buttons with a remark, you can easily speak to him in ways that negate rather than bolster your values. Although many situations might result in value-negating responses, we'd like to focus on the ones that we've found to be most common. Specifically, we want to address the most commonly asked questions and concerns you'll hear from your child. These represent golden opportunities to convey sound money values, and we'd like to help you capitalize on them with the following quiz. As you'll see, the questions are structured in roughly chronological order. Take a look at the questions kids ask, identify how you would answer, and then see if you can identify the value-boosting response.

1. Are we rich?
   a. No.
   b. That's not something you need to worry about.
   c. You better believe it.
   d. We are fortunate to have enough money for ourselves and to be able to help others.

2. Why can't I have that (any toy)?
   a. We can't afford it.
   b. Because if we get you this toy, then you'll want another one and another one after that, and pretty soon you'll turn into the greediest boy in the neighborhood, and you don't want that, do you?
   c. Because it's expensive, and we don't believe in buying everything we see just because we want it. If you really want it, let us know and perhaps you'll receive it for your birthday or another special occasion.
   d. Because I said so.

3. I accidentally took this candy bar from the store without paying for it; what should I do?
   a. I'll take you back to the store right now, and you're going to return it and apologize.
   b. Ordinarily, I'd make you return it, but that store charges ridiculous prices, so this just evens things out.
   c. Let's talk about why you did it. Tell me how you felt and what you thought you were going to accomplish.
   d. I'm going to call the police. You'll have to explain to them what happened.

4. Grandma gave me $100. I'm seven years old, and why can't I spend it the way I want?
   a. We think you could save some of it. Let's sit down and talk about it. What are your ideas?

b. Because it's important for you to start saving for your college education now—college costs a great deal of money.

c. Because you know you're just going to spend it on something you won't care about a year from now.

d. Because you'd hurt Grandma's feelings if you spent the money on junk.

5. **The kids at school are talking about your company and saying we have more money than anybody else. What should I tell them?**

a. Tell them we're not rich.

b. Just ignore them.

c. Explain that although we may be wealthier than other families, we worked hard to be in this position, and if they work hard, they can be wealthy too.

d. You're upset about this, aren't you? What bothers you the most about what they're saying?

6. **All my friends have new cars, and I need a car to get to school. Will you get me one?**

a. I had an old car when I was growing up, and if it was good enough for me, it's good enough for you.

b. I'll get you a new car on the condition that you make the honor roll next semester.

c. Absolutely not. You're not getting a car until you can afford to buy one yourself. There's nothing wrong with taking the bus.

d. I'll help you purchase a safe used car, but we need to sit down and work out the rules, like when you will be home in the evening.

7. Why should I get a summer job? We have plenty of money.

 a. You don't get an allowance during the summer. If you intend to go out with your friends or buy anything for yourself, you need to earn some money.

 b. We do have plenty of money, but we didn't earn it by hanging around the convenience store. You have a lot of growing up to do, and you can start by finding a job.

 c. You don't have to get a summer job, but we think it would be a good idea.

 d. If you don't get a summer job, then you have to do the following tasks around the house.

Answers that build positive values: 1. (d) 2. (c) 3. (a) 4. (a) 5. (d) 6. (d) 7. (a)

As you look at these answers, certain dos and don'ts emerge. Specifically:

- Do be honest; don't tell your child you can't afford something if you really can afford it. Explain why you don't want to buy it.
- Do connect the concept of money with that of responsibility; don't absolve your children of responsibility for their actions simply because you have money.
- Do help them understand that there are limits on spending; don't allow them to spend freely without limits or conditions.
- Do acknowledge your child's negative feelings about money and wealth; don't pretend those feelings are unimportant or will go away.
- Do treat their questions with respect; don't try to shame them into changing their behavior.

SILVER NUGGET

At dinner, ask your kids to talk about what they would do if they suddenly received $1 million, and then tell them what you would do. Use this exercise to help them articulate and examine their financial values.

Avoiding Contradictions Between Words and Deeds

Kids sometimes can read your expressions and actions better than you can read them yourself. From toddlerhood on, kids pick up signals about your money beliefs from the tips you leave for waiters, how you treat the cleaning lady, how you respond to street people, whether you give money to charities, how much you pay your employees, and thousands of other actions.

Don't fool yourself into thinking that your words alone will shape your child's values relative to money. The following example drives this point home. Sam and Matilda, a couple in their late seventies, recently retired with a net worth of more than $5 million. They have two daughters in their forties, and when their children were younger, they talked to them frequently about treating others equally regardless of their wealth, the need for them to work if they wanted to buy things, and the importance of helping those less fortunate than themselves. When they came to see Jon (one of the authors of this book) to talk about their plans to leave a substantial part of their estate to charity, it became clear that they'd sent mixed messages to their girls. This is part of that conversation:

> **Jon:** *Have you thought about giving the money now to your own family foundation and getting your daughters involved?*
>
> **Sam:** *Oh, no. If we put that kind of money in the foundation now, they'd have a good idea of what we're worth. We didn't think it was a good idea for them to know what we have.*
>
> **Jon:** *Well, do your daughters share your interests in philanthropy? We could earmark some of their trust fund income for their favorite charities.*
>
> **Matilda:** *No, we don't want to take anything away from them.*
>
> **Jon:** *Do you want to make your daughters cotrustees of the trusts you are setting up for them?*
>
> **Sam:** *No. They don't know anything about money.*

Throughout their daughters' upbringing, these parents modeled behaviors that contradicted what they told them. Although Sam and Matilda may have talked to their children in ways that communicated good values, they acted in ways that encouraged their children to ignore charitable work, to learn nothing about investments or budgeting, and to believe that Sam and Matilda would always take care of them. They certainly didn't intend to raise daughters who were indulged, self-involved, and helpless when it came to finances, but that's exactly what they did. Sam and Matilda fell into a common modeling trap: their actions contradicted their words. We'd like to share with you the five most common modeling traps and how to avoid them.

1. **Gender-based money management.** In many homes Dad is in charge of the household finances, and Mom has little or no responsibilities in this area. It's no surprise that daughters in these households grow up having difficulty managing their money and, even worse, often feel incompetent or fearful when it comes to

any sort of business transaction involving money. The solution here is to share money management responsibilities equally.

2. **Contradictory messages.** Sam and Matilda's story illustrates one type of contradiction—when parents' actions don't match their stated values. Another type is when parents contradict each other. Going back to our use, management, and acquisition continuum, let's say Dad is a big spender, and Mom is frugal. A child has difficulty trying to reconcile these two contradictory behaviors and may feel a confusion that goes beyond money-use issues; this kid may feel very insecure because Mom accuses Dad of spending all their money or because Dad tells Mom, "You can't take it with you." The right course of action is for spouses to be careful how their money behaviors manifest themselves when kids are around. They may need to moderate their behaviors so they aren't delivering unhealthy and confusing messages to their children.

3. **Token charity.** We've talked to many parents who truly believe in the importance of giving and preach this philosophy to their children. At the same time, however, these kids see very little evidence that their parents practice what they preach. As a result, kids become cynical; as adults they may ignore philanthropy or reject their wealth because it makes them feel guilty. The right course of action here is for parents to become regularly and visibly engaged in philanthropic projects. This can extend to simple, daily actions. For instance, our colleague Jilliene Schenkel, who is an advisor to affluent families and individuals, strongly believes in sharing with those who ask for handouts, but she doesn't want her money to be spent on drugs or alcohol. For years she has purchased gift certificates from McDonald's and carries them in her purse. When she is walking in the city with her children and someone asks her for money, she or her children give them McDonald's gift certificates.

4. **Workaholism.** Children of workaholics tend to grow up either just as work obsessed as their parents or rejecting hard work entirely. When parents seem to value making money over every other activity, it warps a child's perspective about what's important in life. Many workaholic parents don't want to send this message, and they do try and make time for Little League games and school plays. But when they attend these events, they're often talking on cell phones to workmates. We're not suggesting parents shouldn't work hard, but it's important to strike some sort of balance so that children don't feel life is all about making money. The key here is to carve out time with kids each week where work is invisible; no work-related phone calls, E-mails, or discussions are allowed.

5. **Excess.** Again, the point here is not that people shouldn't spend money on luxuries, but if they spend outrageously and in an exhibitionist manner, they should be aware of the message it sends to the children. Buying a red sports car that you enjoy driving is fun; buying five is excessive. A more common example is building a house that is far too large for your family or spending an exorbitant amount on material things to impress people. If you want to make kids feel entitled and superior, this is a good way to do it. Instead, strive to create a balance between luxuries your affluence enables you to afford and things that aren't that expensive. Taking camping vacations, listening to concerts at the park, and going for walks in the woods are all fun and cost relatively little. Doing things with kids that are a lot of fun but don't cost a lot of money gives them a well-rounded perspective on what's available at what price.

Talking to your kids about money is really about being conscious of what money means to you. When you're aware of money's meaning and role in your life, you can do a much better job of talking and acting in ways that are emotionally healthy for your children. Too often, affluent parents don't give their money beliefs a second thought, and the results can be devastating for their sons and daughters. Whether parents fall into the trap of excess, treat money issues as a taboo subject, walk and talk contradictory messages, or deliver money lectures that fall on deaf ears, they inadvertently make mistakes that can haunt their kids for years.

Top-of-mind awareness of your money relationships and values will facilitate your conversations about everything from budgeting to the family's assets. When you keep your money issues and the messages you want to communicate in mind, your words will help shape your child's ideas about money in a positive way.

6

Allowances
Giving Your Child More than Money

Although some specific money interactions with your children will prove important—helping them open their first checking accounts, doing charity work together, helping them save their money for significant purchases—allowances represent a particularly crucial challenge for parents. Few topics generate as much controversy and confusion. Consider just some of the questions and decisions that allowances generate:

- Should your children receive an allowance?
- If so, at what age should it start?
- How much should they get, and should the amount be contingent on doing their chores or maintaining their grades?
- What should they be expected to pay for out of their allowance and what should you continue to pay for?
- Should children receive raises based on age, achieving certain goals, or some other criteria?
- How much freedom should children have to spend their allowances on what they want?
- At what point should parents step in and prevent their children from spending their money on a particular product or service?

Allowances are where the rubber meets the road, where your money values come face to face with the need to talk *with* (and not *to*) your children about money. Allowances are also where unexamined money relationships emerge; the person who is on the far end of the continuum in terms of use gives his child an allowance that is way above the norm; the person who has serious management issues may insist that her child account for every penny of allowance spent. Most children take their allowances seriously. Not only is it a rite of passage when they receive their first allowance, but it continues to carry a great deal of symbolic weight, representing their participation in an adult marketplace. In a very real way, allowances are rehearsals for money relationships later in life when employers (or their own businesses) rather than parents provide them with income.

SILVER NUGGET

Think about your allowance experiences as a child (if they were positive or negative) and whether you want to handle your child's allowance in the same way.

Two Basic Allowance Rules

Some parents refuse to give their children allowances. This may be because they provide their children with whatever they need; why do they need an allowance when they have access to unlimited funds? At the other extreme, some parents don't believe in allowances because they feel it's a handout; if their kids want spending money, they should work for it. We've worked with parents who insist on linking allowances to chores or grades in school, but we've also known couples who view an allowance as an appropriate sharing of the family's resources and don't make it conditional on chores or grades.

A quick look in the dictionary tells us that the word *allowance* is derived from the transitive verb *allow*, which means "to provide or allot a certain amount for a purpose." In other words, if we give our kids an allowance, we are providing them with money for a purpose. What should that purpose be? You're reading this book for ideas to help you raise responsible, well-adjusted kids who know how to manage money. The last thing you want is a spoiled, overindulged, and self-entitled child. Giving your children money via an allowance may seem to encourage a spoiled attitude, but, like affluence, an allowance only has a negative effect if parents refrain from dispensing values along with the money. For instance, an allowance that is significantly above the norm and comes with no strings attached will send the wrong message. You surely don't want to deprive your child of the chance to work hard and achieve goals by handing him everything on a silver platter. If you value accountability and fairness, you're not communicating those values if you regularly hand over a significant amount of money to your child as a reward for his mere existence.

So how much is too much? What sort of strings should be attached to ensure accountability?

We have two basic rules about allowances.

Rule One: All Children Should Receive an Allowance

By the first grade, or perhaps even earlier, your children will find out that other children receive an allowance. When they ask for an allowance and you say no without a valid reason (such as you can't afford it), you will be sending one or more of the following money messages:

- Allowances and money aren't subjects that we talk about in our family.
- The money in our family belongs to the grown-ups, not the kids.
- We share our money with you only if we want to give it to you.

All three messages are inappropriate. Treating allowances and money as subjects that are not talked about in the family simply helps raise financially illiterate children. Treating all money as yours and only sharing it with your kids if you feel like it takes away from the sense of interlocking family responsibilities and privileges that you want to create for your children.

View an allowance as the child's rightful opportunity to share an appropriate portion of the family's resources. This approach gives you the ability to talk rationally and negotiate responsibly with your children about money issues. Handled this way, allowances encourage involvement in the family and can be used to teach children to budget and to deal with consequences.

Rule Two: An Appropriate Allowance Is What You Feel Is Appropriate

If this rule strikes you as wishy-washy, recognize that it's designed to give you the freedom to create an allowance that fits your values and resources as well as the specific items you believe an allowance should cover. In one family, a $5 weekly allowance might be the norm for a ten-year-old, although in another family the norm might be twice as much. Although you don't want to be a slave to your neighborhood's norms—you may not agree with the allowance amounts—you should take them into consideration. We can assure you that your children know how much allowance their friends and neighbors receive. In addition, you may want your thirteen-year-old to pay for her school supplies out of her allowance, though another parent may feel that these supplies are something the parent will supply, and the child should not be asked to pay for them.

Determining what's appropriate is a process you should share with your child. Talk about why she's receiving X dollars and what it should cover. By communicating allowance parameters to your child, you're communicating a rationale that contains your values.

Let's look at how you can communicate values by addressing each of the following allowance questions:

- What do you have to do to get an allowance?
- How is the amount of the allowance determined, and what should it cover?
- When and how can the allowance be renegotiated?
- How much say should parents have over how kids spend their allowances?

What Do You Have to Do to Get an Allowance?

At age three or four, your child starts developing an interest in money and begins to make the connection between giving money

SILVER NUGGET

Conduct an informal survey of parents and kids to determine what the community allowance norm is. But remember, you don't have to keep up with the Joneses. Keep your own values in mind.

and getting something back in return. You will want to start her allowance as she emerges from the "initiative" stage and enters the "industry" stage, as discussed in Chapter 2. Depending on your child's level of maturity, this will occur around age six or seven. As she develops the cognitive ability to understand such abstract concepts as privileges and responsibilities, she's going to want to feel useful and achieve her potential.

Introduce the subject of an allowance when your child has exhibited some form of responsible behavior. Perhaps he helped Mom put items in the shopping basket at the market or she remembered to put away her dolls without being asked. This is the time to sit down and say something along the following lines:

> Dad and I are very impressed about how responsible you have been in (helping at the market, putting your dolls away without being asked, etc.). When kids become old enough to be responsible like you are, they deserve some family privileges. We think you're old enough now to start getting an allowance and share in some of the family's money.

What we didn't include in the above paragraph was just as important as what we did include. Notice that we didn't say a word about chores. Instead, we concentrated on the child's responsible behavior as a member of the family. If your child begins acting out and becomes a behavioral problem at home or at school, you obviously have to deal with the issues. Withholding his allowance may be an option. But linking the allowance to chores is usually a no-win situation. The struggle between parent and child over chores is ongoing and difficult to resolve. Most kids will skip making their beds or taking out the trash at times, and if you punish them by withholding their allowance at each infraction of your chore rules, you're going to turn the allowance into a battlefield where you can never win. You are also going to reinforce the incorrect and inappropriate concept that children should be paid for all the help they give the family.

How Is the Amount of the Allowance Determined, and What Should It Cover?

The amount of your child's allowance depends on a number of factors, the most important of which are your values, what's included in the allowance, and the age of your child. In her wonderful book, *Kiplinger's Dollars and Sense for Kids*, Janet Bodnar lists a number of approaches to setting the amount of an allowance. Some are mechanical formulas, like an allowance equal to their age, so a six-year-old would get $6 a week. The best approach, however, according to Bodnar and others, is to figure out in advance what you expect the allowance to cover and then sit down and discuss the matter openly with your kids. Let's say that when the kids go to the market with you, you've established a family rule that each child can get one treat for himself. Or maybe you have a family ritual of going down to the local yogurt shop after dinner every Wednesday evening for a family treat. Do those treats now get paid for out of the allowance or are you still paying for them? Obviously, the answer is going to affect the amount of your child's allowance. The key to setting the amount is to find that happy medium where the amount is not so low as to be unreasonable but not so high that your child doesn't have to make choices about how to spend his money. In some affluent families children receive such large allowances that they rarely, if ever, have to make tough decisions about purchases or save for weeks or months to make a special purchase.

As your kids get older, allowances should cover more items. By the time your kids are twelve (or even younger), you can include a clothing allowance. Giving your kids a fixed but reasonable amount to spend on clothing provides them with an opportunity to make choices. A variation on the clothing allowance theme is to set a dollar limit on the amount you are willing to pay for certain items and let the kids use their allowance if they want something more expensive. Bodnar set a $50 limit on sneakers. If her children wanted a more expensive pair, they paid the difference out of their allowance. They quickly learned that they really didn't need that $275 pair after all. Other items covered by an allowance as your kids get older can include going to the movies, renting videotapes, and buying CDs and presents for friends.

At the start, the allowance should cover no more than a week. As your child approaches adolescence, it might cover two weeks or even a month. By increasing the intervals, you help your child learn to budget for longer periods. By the time your child is in high school, an allowance should cover a full month. In college, it should probably be based on a full academic quarter or semester.

Although we can't tell you exactly how much to give your children, we can confidently make one prediction: kids tend to run out of money before they run out the week. Expect it. It's the start of learning how to budget. Be understanding and sympathetic. Help them think about how next week they can make the allowance last longer. But don't rescue. It may be difficult not to give your child money if she cannot go to the movie with her friends because of poor budgeting. Resist your impulse to do so, however, because she will learn a tremendous lesson from her mistake. Rescuing sends the worst money message possible: you don't have to be responsible with your money; there's always more money for you.

At the same time, you should provide them with an option for earning some extra money by doing special chores. Again, the allowance shouldn't be tied to routine chores they're expected to do as members of the family. But giving them options to earn money based on additional work above and beyond the call of duty is a terrific learning tool. It mirrors the real world where people who do extra usually get paid extra or receive other rewards (promotions, bonuses, etc.). The link between hard work and additional pay is a good one to make and demonstrates that even in the most affluent of families, you are the one who can rescue yourself.

A good technique here is creating a list of special chores with a specific dollar amount attached to each. This list can include anything beyond the routine tasks that your child is expected to perform, not for an allowance, but because she is a member of the family. Although your children may be expected to shovel snow in winter and rake leaves in fall, they may not be expected to clean out the attic. This is a special project, and thus you might include that on the list. Don't keep this list a secret. Post it somewhere and make your children aware that if they run short of money or want to make more to buy a specific item, they can take advantage of these tasks.

Finally, we don't believe you should base the amount of allowance you give your children on what others in the community are receiving. No doubt, your kids will know the going rate. You should be aware of it and consider it in your calculations, but it may be that you feel the rate is too high or too low, based on your values and what you believe your child's allowance should cover. Making your kid aware of these differences will go a long way toward helping them understand and appreciate your values, and the process of setting the allowance amount is a good catalyst for this awareness.

When and How Can the Allowance Be Renegotiated?

If your children consistently run out of money before the end of their allowance period, you need to take a hard look at what is going on. They may need help in creating a budget and making choices. But it's also possible that the allowance is set unrealistically low and needs to be adjusted. Just as you don't want to send the wrong message about your values by providing your child with too high an allowance, you don't want to set the allowance too low and communicate an inappropriate frugality. If your child's allowance needs to be increased but doing so requires you to deprive yourself, don't do it. But if you don't have to deprive yourself, don't act like a martyr if raising your child's allowance is appropriate.

If your child is consistently running out of money, don't give him a lecture about budgeting and money not growing on trees. Instead, say something like this:

> I've noticed that you've run out of allowance several times recently. How about sitting down and making up a list of what you've been spending your money on and how much you've spent for each item. If you can't remember, maybe you can keep track of what you're spending money on for the next week or two. When you have the list, let's sit down together and go over it. Maybe I can help you with your budget. Or if you don't have enough money, maybe we need to think about either increasing your allowance or finding ways for you to earn extra money.

In this way, you are able to treat the allowance as an appropriate sharing of the family's resources, based on the child's ability to manage the money and the items that the allowance should cover. Your child feels listened to, and you're not in the power struggle that is created when you tie the allowance to chores or grades.

Remember, however, that children can be manipulative, and they may well try to make you feel guilty to increase their allowance. Sometime it pays to double-check. Ruth, a fourteen-year-old living in a wealthy midwestern suburb, was running short of money each week despite the fact that she received a raise from her parents when she entered high school. Ruth complained that she wasn't receiving the same allowance as her friends and that she couldn't spend as much when they went out to eat or to the movies. She told her parents that she was often forced to borrow money from her friends so she could afford to get into the movie and that she was embarrassed; she claimed that her friends thought that her family didn't have as much money as they did and told her she didn't have to pay them back. Ruth's parents felt guilty and were prepared to give her an increased allowance until they talked to the parents of one of her friends, who told them that all the girls had been spending a lot of money at the new video arcade in town. Ruth admitted that this was where a significant percentage of her allowance was going.

How Much Say Should Parents Have Over How Kids Spend Their Allowances?

At about the age of eleven, Craig began spending his entire allowance on heavy-metal music. He would save it up for a few weeks until he had enough to buy a CD and then purchase one that contained lyrics his parents found to be sexist and borderline obscene. They also found the music itself to be loud and irritating. Because Craig had musical talent—he'd been taking guitar lessons for three years—they wanted him to broaden his musical interests and thought this obsession with heavy-metal music was unhealthy. As a result, they forbid him to use his allowance to buy that type of music.

At first Craig tried to reason with them, explaining that rap music was far more violent and obscene and that his heavy-metal disks were tame in comparison. Although his parents knew this was true, they still insisted that Craig was wasting his money on "trash." Then Craig asked, "How can you give me an allowance and then tell me what to spend it on?"

Craig's question is instructive. Parents need to give their children the freedom to spend their allowances as they choose. Invariably, kids will make poor choices. Short of purchasing something that might harm them or others or is illegal (weapons, drugs, etc.), they need to be allowed to make mistakes. Forbidding them to use their money the way they choose is telling them that they can't be trusted, that they are not sufficiently responsible to make buying decisions. This message, repeated often enough, can make them insecure about money and make it difficult as they get older to make money decisions with confidence.

Therefore, when your child starts spending his allowance in ways that you disapprove of, don't deprive him of his freedom of choice or verbally assault his buying decisions. Instead, consider the following tactics:

• **Engage your child in nonjudgmental conversations about his buying choices.** Encourage him to talk about why he likes the heavy-metal CD, the gruesome video game, or the silly toy. Don't turn his purchase into forbidden fruit with intense disapproval. Instead, explain what you find objectionable about the purchase but give him the chance to express why he likes it. This way both of you are able to share ideas and attitudes. By taking the power struggle out of the equation, you also take some of the allure out of a particular purchase.

• **Set limits that don't relate to the allowance.** In other words, define for your child what's unacceptable behavior in your house. Perhaps you might have a rule against playing or singing songs with obscene lyrics or which advocate violence toward women. This limit applies to everyone in the family, not just your child, and it is very specific. Broad, general limits tend to be less effective because they're difficult to enforce and open to interpretation. A limit such as forbidding products with any type of violence would eliminate a significant percentage of television shows, books, and movies, some that may have redeeming aspects. By setting limits that relate to your values, it is also easier to deal with violations of the rules. If Craig buys CDs with obscene lyrics, your response has nothing to do with his allowance. Rather, you are dealing with behavior that is unacceptable in your house, and you can insist that he dispose of the CDs. It is up to Craig to find out whether he can return them to the store for credit or if he just has to throw them away.

SILVER NUGGET

Talk to your spouse about what you'll say to your child when he makes a purchase with his allowance that you don't agree with.

Resist the Reward/Punishment Aspect of Allowances

In many affluent homes, money is equated with what it can buy. There are so many expensive "things" around—luxury cars, beautiful furniture, swimming pools, elaborate home entertainment systems—that it is easy to forget that money can be a means to many ends. Money can be a tool for learning, for art appreciation, for bringing families together, and for doing good in the world. In other words, money is multidimensional, and it's important for kids to learn to view it from this broader perspective.

Allowances that are structured as rewards for doing chores foster a very narrow and crass view of money. Nonetheless, a significant percentage of parents structure their child's allowance in just this way, believing that it's an appropriate method for kids to "earn" money. In reality, we should expect our children to help with chores at home because they're members of our family, not because we pay them. Their membership in the family entitles them to all sorts of privileges, ranging from living in a nice home to going on family vacations. In short, they are allowed to share in the family's resources in exchange for accepting certain responsibilities (such as chores).

If your child is going to become a responsible adult, he needs to know that privileges and responsibilities will be inextricably linked throughout his life. As a member of the family, your child should share in both the privileges and responsibilities that go along with this membership. No doubt you've encountered parents who use the threat of withdrawing an allowance to keep their kids in line: "If you don't come home when I tell you, you're not getting your allowance next week!" Or they use the positive side of the same coin: "Clean up your room every day this week, and we'll double your allowance next week." If you use money to control your child's behavior, you will raise an adult who is controlled by money. He may choose a job he doesn't particularly like because it pays well or become a workaholic because he's obsessed with making more and more money.

If you treat an allowance as part of a system of rewards and punishments, you end up bribing your children to do things that they should be doing either to foster their own sense of self-sufficiency or because they are members of the family. If you tie your children's allowance to behavior, you teach them to associate money with how they act. Do you really want your children to learn the equation "behavior equals money" and place a monetary value on everything they do? When bad behavior equals less money and good behavior equals more money, they don't get a chance to establish an internal sense of right and wrong.

One of the more insidious aspects of a reward/punishment type of allowance is that you're teaching your child that she can buy her way out of some of the responsibilities that go along with family membership by giving up some of the privileges. Let's say that one of your twelve-year-old daughter's chores is to empty the dishwasher every evening after dinner so that the dirty dishes can be stacked in it. She's often too busy and forgets in the rush to go to her girlfriend's house across the street so they can do homework together. So you tell her that you are going to reduce her allowance by $1 each time she forgets to empty the dishwasher. What you have really done is to teach her that she can buy her way out of doing her family responsibilities. From her point of view, going over to her friend's house might be worth giving up a dollar and inconveniencing the parent who has to empty the dishwasher. In fact, you are setting yourself up for a power struggle that you are doomed to lose. After a number of allowance deductions, you may wind up withholding her entire allowance out of frustration with her "forgetfulness." What do you do when she tells you that she's decided not to do any chores around the house because money isn't that important to her?

Although it may be easier in the short run to attempt to use an allowance as a behavior modification tool, in the long run your child will pay for your avoidance of the real issues. In this instance, the proper approach is to deal with the situation that is interfering with your daughter's carrying out a family responsibility. Looked at from this viewpoint, the answer is simple: you might say, "When dinner is finished, you can go over to Sue's house to do homework after you have emptied the dishwasher. If it takes too much time to do it after dinner, do you think you ought to get up a few minutes earlier in the morning and empty the dishwasher before going to school or perhaps get home a few minutes earlier and empty the dishwasher before dinner starts?" By handling the situation in this manner, you are not equating behavior with money; you are neither punishing her nor treating her as a subordinate to whom you are giving orders. Instead, you are helping her to recognize consequences—not being able to go to Sue's house to study until the dishwasher is empty—and identify reasonable alternatives: emptying the dishwasher in the morning or before dinner.

It's also unwise to tie allowances to grades, athletic performance, or any other activity. Think back to Erik Erikson's fourth stage of child development, the period of "industry versus inferiority" that begins about age six or seven, which is also about the time that children should start receiving an allowance. Children want to feel useful and achieve their potential at this point in their lives. Your child should be doing homework and getting good grades for himself to engender a sense of personal achievement and satisfaction, not to earn money from you. You should reward your child with praise for doing well in school or making the winning touchdown. Perhaps an extragood report card deserves the entire family going out to celebrate at his favorite restaurant. But you certainly don't want your child to learn to associate good grades with money. Doing so dampens internal motivation and shifts the focus to external rewards.

7

Diversity

How to "Unshelter" Your Child

If you are raising your children in a relatively homogeneous community and are sending them to schools, camps, and other activities where most of the children come from similar backgrounds, encouraging them to value the differences in people can be a challenge. Many children are growing up in suburbs where the vast majority of the community is affluent—where everyone has at least two cars, and summer camp is a part of the routine. Some affluent children growing up in urban areas attend private schools where the homogeneous traits of the student population are even more pronounced. Although there may be ethnic diversity, there is sometimes little socioeconomic diversity. Kids growing up in this type of environment tend to take certain luxuries for granted. They assume that everyone has a computer, a cleaning service, and his own bedroom because the vast majority of their friends enjoy these luxuries.

If parents simply accept this socioeconomic sameness, their children may grow up looking down on others who appear different. This may not take the form of overt prejudice against minorities or blatant snobbery against those who have less money, but it can manifest itself in other ways. Imagine if your child never made a friend whose parents were not of your same financial standing or avoided situations where he might have to "mix" with people who were unlike himself. What if his choice of careers was dictated more by a desire to do what those of his "group" chose to do rather than what really turns him on? We know of more than one child of wealthy parents who went into the family business or became a doctor or lawyer when what they really wanted to do was work with handicapped kids or be a potter. None of these prejudicial attitudes may even be conscious. They often evolve subtly from an insular upbringing that instills prejudice against those who have less.

The irony of all this, of course, is that our world is becoming increasingly diverse. Although we may be raising our children in homogeneous ways, work and social environments are far more diverse than in the past. For our children to thrive as adults both in their careers and in their relationships, they must learn to appreciate people whose backgrounds and behaviors seem "foreign" to them. When children learn to value economic diversity, they also learn to value other types of diversity. When a child realizes that someone with less money has just as much to offer (intellectually and emotionally, as a student and as a friend) as wealthier kids, he learns a tremendous life lesson.

As we'll see, this lesson in diversity is one that all parents are well equipped to teach.

Recognizing the Gap Between Haves and Have-Nots

It's astonishing how many children in well-to-do homes lack a basic understanding of the economic facts of life. Specifically, they don't understand that they possess far more than most other children or that, financially speaking, they represent a very small segment of society. One of the easiest things for even the youngest of children to learn is that great economic disparity exists in the world. This may not seem like a revelation to you or me, but it can have a profound impact on the way a child views the people he meets. When a child realizes what he has versus what other children have—when he grasps what his family is able to buy and enjoy versus other families—he is beginning to appreciate economic diversity. Though this is only a first step, it's an important one. Many children never learn these basic economic facts and as a result never have a foundation for appreciating those who have less. They grow up with a vague sense that there is disparity but no specific, deeply felt consciousness of the fact. They may become adults without ever having given much thought to the struggles a poor family must go through or the way a lower-middle-class family has to forsake activities and privileges people in their community take for granted. Appreciation of these differences, however, paves the way for valuing people who come from different economic and social backgrounds.

To help your child develop a sense of financial perspective from an early age, try this exercise with him as early as age five:

SILVER NUGGET

To find out your child's level of awareness of the gap between the haves and have-nots, ask your child if he believes most of the people in your city (or state) have the same types of toys as he does, the same ability to go on nice vacations, and the same opportunity to go to college. If your child is unaware of the gap, this chapter offers ways to increase that awareness.

ather the following items: ten large pieces of paper numbered one to ten, ten small pieces of paper numbered one to ten, twenty cookies (preferably soft oatmeal cookies, though any cookies that won't crumble into tiny bits when broken are fine), a platter, and ten people. If you can't round up some of the neighborhood kids and their parents to participate with your family, use your kids' action figures or dolls as substitutes.

2. Place the platter, with ten of the cookies, in the center of a large table. Set the large pieces of paper around the table in sequence, starting with one and ending with ten.

3. Using the small pieces of paper, have everyone pick a number and have them stand around the table in front of the paper with their number on it. Explain that each person now represents 10 percent of the people in America and that the ten cookies represent all of the wealth in the country.

4. Start off by telling them that they are going to look at how the wealth in America was owned twenty-five years ago. Have the kid standing at number one take five of the cookies. Have the other nine kids, representing 90 percent of the population, divide the remaining five cookies among themselves. Explain that twenty-five years ago, the wealthiest 10 percent of Americans owned 50 percent of the nation's wealth. The remaining 90 percent of Americans shared the remaining 50 percent of the country's wealth.

5. Now ask the child with five cookies the following questions:

- How does it make you feel to have half the wealth of the country?
- How do you think the other nine people feel about having to share the remaining half of the wealth?

- Does having more wealth make you a better person than the other nine? Does it make you smarter and better looking or merely richer?

6. Ask the other nine children the following questions:

- How do you feel about sharing the remaining half of the wealth in the country?
- Does having less money make you "worse" than the one kid with half the wealth?
- Are you uglier, more stupid, or less deserving or do you just have less money?
- Do you want people to judge you based on the money you have?
- Are you your money or is money simply one aspect of what you have?

7. Place ten more cookies on the platter. Explain that the year is now the current one and that in the last twenty-five years, the gap between the haves and the have-nots has increased. Today, the wealthiest 10 percent of Americans own 70 percent of the nation's wealth. So, this time the child representing the wealthiest 10 percent gets seven of the cookies.

8. Have the remaining nine kids, representing 90 percent of the population, share the remaining three cookies. But this time tell them that they are going to divide up the remaining three cookies the way that the remaining 30 percent of the wealth in America is actually owned.

9. For you to do that, you need to look at the following chart and then explain it as follows:

The top 1 percent of Americans own 40 percent of the nation's wealth. The next 9 percent own 30 percent. This means that 10 percent of the people own 70 percent of the nation's wealth. This leaves 30 percent of the nation's wealth to be divided among 90 percent of the population! But here the numbers become stark. Of that 30 percent, 29.8 percent is owned by Americans in the eleventh to sixtieth percentiles. That means that only .2 percent of the wealth of this country is left to be divided among the bottom 40 percent of our populace. Their share of the chart is so small it can only be approximated by the small line emanating from the right side of the chart.

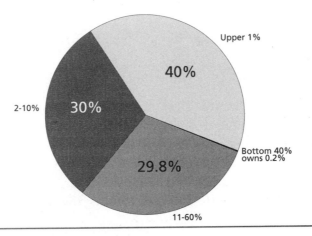

Distribution of wealth in the United States.

10. Tell the nine people who share the three cookies to cut each cookie into ten pieces. (Hint: cut the cookie in half first and then cut each half into five pieces.) Now they have thirty pieces. Take one piece and break off about one-fifth. Give that tiny piece to the four people standing at places seven through ten. Explain that, today, the poorest 40 percent of Americans—well more than 100 million people—literally get to share a crumb! You might also mention that thirty million of them are living under the official

poverty line and forty-two million of them don't have health insurance. The balance of the cookies go to the five people standing at places two though six, who represent the eleventh through sixtieth percent of Americans.

We've found that children as young as five get something valuable out of this exercise. Although they may not understand all the statistics, they grasp the basic lesson. For older children this exercise often catalyzes a lot of questions and interest in the subject of wealth. The following are discussion points you might want to use with this older group:

• The rich in America are not simply getting richer; the poor are getting poorer. Between 1983 and 1998, the net worth of the wealthiest 40 percent of American families increased an average of 20 percent, with the wealthiest 1 percent increasing its net worth by 42.2 percent. During the same period, the net worth of the poorest 40 percent of American families decreased by 76 percent. (Source: Edward N. Wolff, "Recent Trends in Wealth Ownership, 1983–1998," *Jerome Levy Economics Institute Report*, June 2000, vol. 10, no. 2.)

• The increasing gap between the haves and have-nots is also shown in income statistics. Between 1979 and 1998, real income of the wealthiest 20 percent of American families increased an average of 38 percent. Real income of the poorest 20 percent of American families decreased an average of 5 percent. (Source: U.S. Census Bureau, Historical Income Tables, Table F-3. Available through www.census.gov.)

• A useful way of illustrating income disparity in a way that older children can appreciate is to translate dollars into hours spent earning the money to pay for different items. The U.S. minimum wage is currently $5.15. A single parent with one child working at minimum wage forty hours per week for fifty weeks a year will gross $10,300, which is under the federal poverty guideline of $11,250 for a family of two. To purchase a $149.95 pair of Nike basketball shoes for a teenage son, this parent must work slightly less than thirty hours, or approximately three and one-half days. A professional earning $150,000 a year only needs to work two hours to buy the same pair of shoes.

Doesn't Everyone Live This Way?

Our kids need to understand, both intellectually and emotionally, how affluence provides them with advantages that are not available to many others. If they don't learn this lesson, they are likely to believe that their success in life is entirely attributable to their own innate abilities and that people with less money have only themselves to blame for their misfortune. Such an attitude breeds elitism and kills empathy.

To put a human face on this issue, let's look at Timothy.

Timothy's a nice kid. He's eleven years old and in sixth grade. Timothy's father is a successful entrepreneur. His mother quit her job when Timothy was born so she could be a full-time mom. They are devoted parents who make a conscious effort not to let their affluence spoil their son. Timothy attends a good, local private school and is doing well. Most of the time Timothy remembers to do his chores around the house without being asked. His friends live in the neighborhood, and they, too, are good kids; they aren't into drugs and don't get into trouble. Like most of his friends, Timothy has a TV, telephone, and computer in his room. Timothy and his friends believe that they represent the average American kid. And why not? After all, their parents don't tell them differently, and their only immediate measure of comparison is one another and what they see on TV. But they don't see the big picture.

That's why Timothy and his friends made fun of the way a scholarship kid at their school dresses, laughing at his out-of-style pants and his scuffed penny loafers. The notion of hand-me-downs is unknown to them; they would never wear the "used" clothes of an older sibling. It's also why Timothy sulked when his parents told him they were not going to give him $100 to buy a ticket for a rock concert. Timothy was incredulous. His parents had bought him tickets for concerts in the past (albeit ones that cost less), and his two closest friends were going to the concert. Timothy honestly believed his parents were being unfair and was furious that they were depriving him of what he felt was his right.

Intellectually and emotionally, Timothy is sheltered. Although he may have driven through a poor neighborhood in the car or seen starving Ethiopians on the news, these represent anomalies to Timothy. The world also contains Siamese twins and poison-ous lizards, but they are not part of his everyday consciousness. He just doesn't give people outside of his economic group much thought. As a result, children like Timothy don't understand how the vast majority of people truly live. In their sheltered envi-ronment, they rarely, if ever, have to deal with issues of anxiety and uncertainty surrounding money. Because they have not had to deal with these issues, they lack empathy with those who do. Instead, their environment leads them to divide the world into winners and losers. Because they consider their environment to be "normal" and status and money are linked in their minds with being "normal," they feel they deserve what they have. Those with less tend to be dismissed as unimportant and undeserving.

SILVER NUGGET

To get an idea whether your child is aware of the issues created by economic diversity, for the next week notice every time your child makes comments about individuals or groups that are in bad shape economically: do the comments express sympathy or unacceptance?

The School Curriculum and the Societal Curriculum

Timothy and his friends need to understand that they aren't better; their parents simply have more money! Unfortunately, society, the schools, and the media often combine (sometimes unintentionally) to teach Timothy and his friends that having money is the best thing that can happen to them. In *The Children Are Watching*, Carlos E. Cortes states that young people's beliefs and feelings about human diversity are formed by two primary sources: the "school curriculum" and the "societal curriculum." As the name implies, the school curriculum is the formal educational system. The societal curriculum is a parallel, informal, but highly influential source of education about diversity.

Of all the messages provided by the school curriculum and reinforced by the societal curriculum, perhaps the most pernicious are classism and competitive individualism.

Classism is the process of treating groups of people differently because of their class background. In essence, classism consists of creating stereotypes of people based on an identifiable characteristic, such as sex, race, or economic status. Although it would be nice to think that the educational system combats classism, historically it actually encourages it. The September 1970 *Harvard Educational Review* reported a three-year study by Ray Rist in which he determined that schoolteachers' expectations about the academic potential of their students were based almost entirely on the racial and socioeconomic status of the children. The teachers used such expectations to divide their classes into groups that they anticipated would succeed or fail. Rist's study disclosed that, during the school year, the teachers devoted more of their time to the groups that they expected would succeed. By spending less time with the groups they expected to fail, the teachers created a self-fulfilling prophecy in which a measurable achievement gap emerged between the two groups.

In *Open Minds to Equality*, Nancy Schniedewind and Ellen Davidson define *competitive individualism* as

> the notion that an individual's successes or failures in life depend solely on her or his own efforts and merits, and that each person has an equal chance to compete and succeed. This discounts the powerful influence of race, gender, class, or any other aspects of a person's social identity, on a person's chances for opportunity and success.

Competitive individualism helps to reinforce the stereotypes created by classism. If everyone has an equal chance on a level playing field, winners and losers obviously get what they deserve. Competitive individualism is unquestionably encouraged by the school curriculum. Schniedewind and Davidson point to the typical science fair as an apt example: "Typically science fairs are competitive, with awards often going to the students whose parents were able to give them the most support."

But the societal curriculum is an even bigger booster of competitive individualism. A wonderful example of this is found in

Dinesh D'Souza's *The Virtue of Prosperity: Finding Values in an Age of Techno-Affluence.* To D'Souza, poverty "is no longer a significant problem in America." D'Souza embraces the comments of Peter Huber, whom he describes as a "new-economy enthusiast," who argues that "humanity finally triumphed over material scarcity, in America, at the close of the twentieth century. . . . Oh yes, we do still have richer and poorer all about us but that's relative—it's poverty that has ended in our time, not inequality." D'Souza argues that the thirty million living under the poverty line really aren't poor: 98 percent have refrigerators, they are "better housed, better clothed, and better fed than average Americans were half a century ago," and, anyway, "poor people often grossly underreport their incomes, no doubt to maintain their eligibility for federal programs." In D'Souza's worldview, not only are poor people not poor—they have refrigerators, after all—but they also lie about their income. This type of worldview allows one to dismiss poverty as nonexistent while simultaneously arguing that the poor deserve their situation.

Classism and competitive individualism conspire to create kids who don't see the world clearly. They don't really "get" the fact that the child in their school from a disadvantaged background

SILVER NUGGET

If your children are at least age twelve, rent the movie *Stand and Deliver,* which reveals the immense obstacles a class of economically disadvantaged Los Angeles students had to overcome to do well in math. Watch the movie with your children and ask them to share their feelings about what they saw.

can't afford private lessons, has to devote part of his studying time to caring for a younger sibling, and has parents who lack the time or ability to help him with his homework. Most parents don't want to raise their kids to be elitists or children who naively believe that everyone has an equal opportunity to succeed. If parents don't intervene, however, their children are likely to harbor elitist attitudes and naive beliefs.

Eight Things We Can Do to Teach Our Children About Diversity

To counteract the ubiquitous messages of classism and competitive individualism, we must learn to help our children value people for their character, who they are (not what they have), the obstacles they have surmounted, and what they have accomplished with their lives. There are many ways to do this, and the actions you take will depend in part on the type of person you are and type of child you have. Still, the following eight suggestions will be useful for most parents concerned about raising a diversity-sensitive child.

1. **Clarify your own values about diversity and determine whether your actions are consistent with your values.** We're making the assumption that most readers of this book will value both socioeconomic and racial diversity, but you should give some thought to your feelings about these issues. Assuming you consider diversity to be an important value, review your actions of the past year with the following questions in mind:

- Do you treat household help and tradespeople with respect?
- Do you ever make derogatory remarks about people from less-affluent segments of society, referring to them as "trailer trash" or other negative names?

- Are your friends primarily from the same socioeconomic group? Are the people you invite over to the house (and that your child sees you with) from the same or diverse groups?
- Have you ever explained the economic facts of life to your child? Do you make an effort to communicate that a very different world exists beyond your neighborhood and that it's important to be aware of this world?

2. Make the connection between your earnings and the cost of products and services related to your child. If you make $150,000 a year and spend $15,000 on school tuition, you can explain to your child that education is so important in your family that you work more than a month every year just to earn the money for tuition. Then talk about how someone who only earns $30,000 a year would have a difficult time spending half his salary just on school tuition. Doing this a few times a year will help your child comprehend that not every child's family can afford the things her family can. Linking the cost of something relevant to your child with the percentage of your salary helps drive home the fact that people have vastly different purchasing power. You can use the Money Pie of Life here (see Chapter 4) to explain the concept graphically to your children. Be sure to emphasize that earning more than someone else does not make you better than him; you simply have more discretionary income.

3. Play the cookie game with your children, as well as the lemon game (for children ages eight and under). Gather four or five kids and give each one of them a lemon. Ask them to find out something special about their lemon. Maybe it's a slight discoloration or a scratch on the skin. Take the lemons back, put them in a bowl and ask the children to locate their own lemon. Even four-year-olds usually have little trouble in locating their own lemon. Now take the lemons, peel them and put them back in the bowl and ask children to locate their lemon. Obviously, they won't be able to. Explain to them that people are just like lemons: once you get rid of the outside—clothes, hair, and the color of their skin—we're all alike. This simple lesson in valuing people for themselves rather than for what they have is something that will resonate with most kids. Now go make lemonade with the kids so that you don't waste the lemons!

4. **Educate yourself about diversity training.** Many of us have had little or no experience in helping others appreciate diversity. We may find it awkward to talk to our children about this subject or feel we're going about it wrong. An easy solution to this problem is to read some good books on diversity training. We highly recommend the book *Open Minds to Equality*, by Nancy Schniedewind and Ellen Davidson. In addition to socioeconomic diversity, it covers race, religion, age, and how to teach these topics to others. Another excellent source of information on diversity is the Anti-Defamation League's "World of Difference Institute," a program started in Boston in 1985 by the Anti-Defamation League and WCVB-TV. The "Classroom of Difference" program is the heart of the institute, developed to address diversity issues in prekindergarten through twelfth-grade classes. Although directed to elementary- and secondary-school teachers—some 350,000 have participated in the program to date—the materials are equally useful for parents. *ADL Resources for Classroom and Community*, a free catalog of books, videos, and other resources to teach diversity, is available from the ADL website, www.adl.org, and some public libraries.

5. **Model diversity-conscious viewing, listening, and reading habits.** Studies have shown that the amount and kind of television that young children are exposed to depends considerably on the amount and kind of viewing their parents do. In "Television and Socialization of Young Children," a study conducted in the late 1980s by the University of Kansas Center for Research on the

Influences of Television on Children, Aletha C. Huston and John C. Wright point out that parents' viewing habits and preferences are a powerful source of modeling and early exposure to television for young children. The types of programs that parents and children view together are guided by the parents' tastes, not those of the children. Therefore, include in your media regimen a range of documentaries and history-based television programs, newspapers, and books that expose kids to different cultures, economic groups, and lifestyles.

SILVER NUGGET

Go through the television guide and place a "D" for diversity next to programs that, from their descriptions or your experience, provide the sort of viewing you want to encourage.

6. **Become media spin doctors.** Don't just sit there in silence when you and your child are watching a television program that raises diversity issues. These are great teachable moments, and you can take advantage of them by providing a values-based spin on a given show. This doesn't mean lecturing but simply pointing out an issue your child may miss or not understand. For instance, if you're watching a show in which one character is acting like a snob, note that fact and ask your child if he knows anyone like that. During a commercial or after the show, you can talk about why snobs act the way they do.

7. **Teach your child the difference between generalizations and stereotypes.** Stereotyping is something that many

affluent children fall into. They hear their friends make stereotypical remarks and naturally copy that behavior. They look at a group of kids from the "other" side of the tracks, see they don't get great marks in school, and stereotype them as "lazy." Although some of them might be lazy, others are handicapped by some of the issues we discussed earlier—lack of resources for private lessons, uneducated or non-English-speaking parents, other time-consuming responsibilities at home, and so on.

Our children need to develop the ability to ask themselves whether beliefs they hold about groups are generalizations that might correctly apply to *some* of the members of the group or stereotypes that unrealistically apply to *all*. Talk about the difference between *some* and *all* with your children, and ask them for examples of both that they've heard at school.

8. Widen your children's horizons. If diversity is important to you, look for opportunities to expose your children to different socioeconomic groups in an intelligent and caring manner. Here are some options you might consider:

- Select schools that cater to socioeconomic diversity. Many schools, both public and private, have programs in which community involvement is part of the day-to-day school curriculum. Talk to teachers and students about the program before making up your mind about a school.

- Look for opportunities to expose your children to socioeconomic diversity. If you stand with your back to the Pacific Ocean in Malibu, you are at the western edge of a golden rectangle of roughly 150 square miles in size that encompasses most of the high-net-worth bedroom communities of metropolitan Los Angeles: Beverly Hills, Brentwood, Bel Air, Santa Monica, and Encino. It is possible to be born, live your entire life, and be buried without leaving the rectangle. Similar enclaves exist throughout the country. If you are a parent raising a family in such an area, unless you make a conscious effort, the only exposure to socioeconomic diversity that your child will receive will be limited to the housekeeper and sales staff at local stores.

- Take trips that encourage exposure to other cultures and types of people. Go to different places each year, and don't stay at hotels that isolate you from people who actually live in the area. Make an effort to get your child to interact with people in the community, and avoid spending all your time on tourist activities that provide little exposure. A young couple we know alternates high-end luxury hotels with less-expensive hotels when they travel so their children do not automatically assume they will always be staying at only the very best.

- Get involved in a local community organization that provides entrée to socioeconomic diversity in your area. A good place to start is with the Funding Exchange, a network of fifteen community foundations that provide funding for community-based efforts addressing a wide range of social problems, with an emphasis on grassroots organizing. Their website is www.fex.org. We'll talk more about the Funding Exchange in Chapter 8.

- Take a Volunteer Vacation. Several years ago, Bill McMillon, author of *Volunteer Vacations*, attended a speech by psychiatrist Karl Menninger. Menninger was asked what advice he would give to a person who felt a nervous breakdown coming on. His reply was "Lock up your house, go across the railway tracks, find someone in need, and do something to help that person." As McMillon pointed out, it didn't matter to Menninger which side of the tracks you lived on; you help yourself by going across the tracks and helping others. *Vol-*

unteer Vacations, now in its seventh edition, lists 250 organizations throughout the world that offer an opportunity to combine vacations with helping others. Consider the following examples:

- The British Trust for Conservation Volunteers in Oxfordshire sponsors activities as diverse as repairing footpaths in the Scottish Highlands and radio-tracking wolves in Slovakia.
- Global Citizens Network is looking for volunteers, in venues ranging from South Dakota and New Mexico to Guatemala and Nepal, who want to live with local families while working on community development projects, such as building health clinics, renovating a youth center, and developing materials for a day-care center. The only special skills needed are "a willingness to experience and accept a new culture."
- Malta Youth Hostels Association Work Camps in Pawla, Malta, needs volunteers for two weeks to three months to work in youth hostels as well as other youth and charitable organizations.
- Quest, in Mt. Rainier, Maryland, works with agencies to provide assistance to the homeless, children with AIDS, and abandoned children living in an orphanage in Tijuana.
- World Horizons International in Bethlehem, Connecticut, sponsors programs in rural Alaska, Africa, the Caribbean, Central and South America, and Samoa. Programs include repairing and building local community facilities, establishing day camps for children, and working with senior citizens.

Raising a child who appreciates the economic, social, and cultural diversity in our world is an important task for all parents, but it's especially important for parents in affluent communities. It's amazingly easy for kids to be ignorant of this diversity and develop a condescending and uninformed attitude toward groups who don't have as much as they do. Fortunately, it's just as easy to prevent or correct this attitude with the eight tactics suggested here.

8

Give and You Shall Receive

I f you're going to raise responsible children in an affluent environment, philanthropy must be part of your value system. You
need to introduce your children to both the concept and practice
of helping others at an early age. In the words of Peter Karoff, the
founder and chairman of the Philanthropic Initiative, Inc., a nonprofit organization formed in 1989 to support and encourage the
growth of strategic philanthropy, the only way to transfer philanthropic values to your children is to "make it as experiential as
possible. If you want your kids to play in the sandbox, they have
to have sand."

When we refer to philanthropy, we're referring to giving in the
broadest possible sense. We deliberately are not using the word
charity, which comes from the Latin *caritas*, meaning "from the
heart." Charity generally involves voluntary gifts of money to
those in need or to organizations that help needy people. *Philanthropy*, on the other hand, is the combination of two Greek words
(*philein*, to love, and *anthropos*, man) and refers to a desire to help
mankind. We are using this term to encompass all forms of activity and endeavor that help make the world a better place in which
to live.

Philanthropy certainly isn't an endeavor limited solely to the
affluent. Jilliene T. Schenkel, an advisor in Southern California to

families and individuals who want to prepare the "next generation" for the transfer of intergenerational family wealth, has
observed that "the responsibility to help others isn't tied to
money; it's tied to existence. Money is incidental; if you have it,
it becomes a tool. Affluence is simply an additional opportunity
to make the world better."

In an increasingly secular society, many of us have lost this philanthropic impulse. An obligation to others is recognized by all of
the world's great religions. Christianity ("Love your neighbor as
yourself"), Judaism ("What is hateful unto you, don't do unto
your neighbor"), and Islam ("None of you believes [completely]
until he loves for his brother what he loves for himself") all give
us versions of the Golden Rule. Christianity provides us with
tithing; Judaism gives us *Tzedakah*, charity, and *Tikkum Olam*, the
requirement that all people have a responsibility to work with
God in perfecting the world; and *Zakaat*, or almsgiving, is one of
the Five Pillars on which Islam is based.

As our society becomes more secular, your children may not be
as influenced by these cultural and religious precepts as prior generations. As a result, it's up to you to communicate them, whether
or not you are formally engaged with these religious traditions. If
you do, your children will benefit as they are moving through the
developmental stages.

SILVER NUGGET

Consider how religion or spirituality influenced your
attitudes toward philanthropy as a child. What were
you taught? Do your children share the same attitudes
toward philanthropy that you did as a child?

The Psychological Impact of Philanthropy

Alfre Woodard, the Emmy- and Golden Globe–winning actress and cofounder of Artists for a New South Africa, notes in the preface to the book *Robin Hood Was Right* by Chuck Collins and Pam Rogers that "generosity links us, beyond time and place, to people of conscience and action everywhere who have made our world freer, kinder, and more just. Philanthropy and activism are a gift to one's self. By giving, we lessen our own cynicism and alienation."

Involvement in philanthropy allows our children to navigate the developmental stages in a more meaningful way. Remember, by age six or seven, children are entering the "industry" stage, where they want to feel useful. Philanthropy helps build a sense of accomplishment—"I'm helping others"—while counteracting the sense of superiority or privilege that can inhibit industry. In the teenage years, when children are dealing with "identity versus role confusion," philanthropy lets them know who they are and helps them to define their social roles. Assisting others—and the satisfaction that comes from offering that assistance with joy and respect for those receiving it—confers a sense of mastery over life. By giving of themselves and their time, children find a satisfying answer to the question "Who am I without my family's money?" Equally important, philanthropy provides teenagers with an activity that can be shared with the entire family.

Affluent children can be given so much that they focus on their own needs to the exclusion of others. Philanthropy helps shift this focus. It demonstrates that they are not just the recipient of giving but have the capacity for giving as well. They learn that satisfaction can be derived from money not just because it enables them to buy what they want, but because it can create better lives for others. Although children may intellectually grasp this concept, they also need to experience it as a participant in the philanthropic process. Seeing the results of a good deed done has an emotional impact that won't be forgotten. It is an empowering experience, especially for younger children, who sometimes feel as if they aren't able to impact the world in a significant manner. When they work at a soup kitchen and ladle out food to a homeless man or when they distribute gifts at a children's hospital, they gain a profound sense of their place in the world. They *feel* the power of doing good, and it's a great antidote to whatever feelings of privilege and greed they may develop growing up surrounded by material goods.

Finally, philanthropy is a meaningful activity. This is no small point considering that teenagers especially often view the world from an existential perspective. At the most extreme, they adopt a cynical pose, professing to believe in nothing except their own immediate needs. Philanthropic endeavors contradict this notion of a meaningless existence. When adolescents perform services for others who are less well off, they realize that they possess the capacity to do something meaningful, and by extension they learn they can live meaningful lives. This can start the process whereby teenagers shuck off their cynicism and begin to mature into responsible adults.

Roadblocks to Family Philanthropy

As logical as our arguments about philanthropy might be, many parents still refrain from making good works a part of the family routine. Many well-to-do families who could easily afford the relatively small commitment of money and time philanthropy requires avoid making that commitment. We've found that three obstacles stand in the way of family philanthropy.

First, some parents have a dysfunctional money relationship in the area of use. They hate to part with any of their money, whether it's for a good cause or not. They model tightfisted behaviors, refusing to involve themselves or their children in philanthropy because of the financial cost. Some of these people, of course, are able to change their use behaviors (at least regarding family philanthropy) when they realize that this is an important child-raising activity. Like Ebenezer Scrooge, they wake up to the realization that it's better to share money than to count it. Others, whose dysfunctional relationship with use is more deeply rooted, may benefit from therapy.

Second, some people believe that philanthropy begins (and ends) at home. They may not have a psychological problem with spending money, but they do have a problem spending money on those less fortunate than themselves. They may have certain prejudices about disadvantaged members of our society that cause them to avoid any type of philanthropy. It's difficult for adults to move away from these prejudices quickly or easily.

The previous two obstacles can be difficult to overcome. The third one, however, is both easier to surmount and much more common. Many people simply don't know how to become involved in philanthropy, both as individuals and as parents. Although everyone understands the process of giving, the process of becoming "productively" involved is less well understood. Let's examine some useful beginning points.

Getting Started

Two missteps sometimes occur on the road to philanthropy, and well-to-do people are most likely to make these mistakes.

First, don't limit your philanthropy to writing checks. Giving money to worthy organizations should be a component of your philanthropy, but hands-on volunteerism will be more soul satisfying, both to you and your children.

Second, don't be a patronizing volunteer. There is no such thing as bad philanthropy. After all, no matter what your motive, your money will eventually help someone. But when it comes to being a volunteer, it is possible to do more harm than good. Being a volunteer is not for everyone. We must be able to separate the people we are working with from the problems that philanthropy and social activism seek to solve. The problems we are addressing may be poverty, homelessness, substance abuse, or lack of education. But the people we deal with must be approached with respect. Nothing causes more ill will than the volunteer who parachutes in with all the answers, devotes eight hours of his superior intellect and social standing to helping the downtrodden, and retires to the church, synagogue, or country club to pat himself on the back. If you feel that you cannot approach hands-on philanthropy with a sense of respect for the persons you are helping, it's far better to stick with writing checks. As fifteenth-century playwright Pierre Corneille put it, "The manner of giving is worth more than the gift."

With these two warnings in mind, the first and easiest thing to do is decide how much of the family's resources (both time and money) should be devoted to philanthropic activities annually. Although it's fine for children to participate in this decision, parents should obviously designate a reasonable amount given their income. The actual amount of money given doesn't really matter. Some people believe in tithing—giving ten percent of their income to church and charity. Others vary the amount given annually, based on their income. You should choose a percentage or amount that's comfortable for you.

Just deciding on this amount and telling your child that you're going to be giving to a good cause isn't sufficient, especially if your child is young. Writing a check to charity is too abstract a concept for a four- or five-year-old. Young children have difficulty dealing with abstractions and need concrete experiences. For this reason, involvement in a volunteer activity is key. Children are not born with an impulse to help make the world a better place to live. It takes parental modeling and active participation for this impulse to come alive in our children.

You have many opportunities to start modeling philanthropic behavior when your children are three or four years old. Sherry, for instance, began modeling this behavior when her daughter, Tracy, was only three years old. She explained to Tracy that there were many children whose mommies and daddies didn't have the money to buy them toys. (You need to keep the explanation simple at this age. A three-year-old won't understand the whys of poverty.) Sherry suggested that Tracy gather up the toys she was "too big for" and put them in a bag. They drove over to a shelter run by a local church, and Tracy carried the bag in. Tracy is now five, and several times a year they engage in the mother-daughter activity of filling up a bag with old toys and driving to the shelter. Tracy occasionally changes her mind on the drive over and decides that she really isn't finished with a toy and wants to keep it. Sherry always agrees and suggests that next time Tracy might want to give that toy away, too.

Robert and Jane's eight- and ten-year-olds attend a Jewish day school that helps support a local food bank. On Friday each child brings two cans of food to school for the food bank. To make the food bank come alive for the children, their parents decided that the entire family would donate a few hours every week to work there. They bring their four-year-old along, and she helps stack canned goods on the lower shelves.

If you are involved with a nonprofit organization, bringing your child to a board meeting can be an eye-opening experience. Anne is very active in several local organizations. She recently asked her twelve-year-old son if he would like to attend an evening board meeting, after which they could get an ice cream cone on the way home. After the meeting was over, he wondered why it had been held after dinner rather than during the day. He was surprised to find out that all of the people at the meeting were unpaid volunteers with jobs during the day who were donating their time to help the organization. Not only did the experience make volunteerism a living concept for him, but it also turned into a teachable moment where the two discussed Anne's involvement with various philanthropic organizations. Anne discovered later that her son was making a quarterly contribution to the organization from his allowance without telling her.

Getting a teenager started on a philanthropic project may be a bit more challenging than a younger child. In fact, when we conduct our workshops, we're frequently asked how to convince a reluctant fourteen- or fifteen-year-old to get involved in good causes. What can you do at this age to make a child view philanthropy as an important family value? The question always reminds us of when we attended an open house at one of our children's schools many years ago. We were in the music teacher's room, and one of the fathers asked the teacher what he could do to get his fifteen-year-old to listen to classical music, rather than rap music. The teacher asked the father what kind of music he listened to at home with his son, and the father replied that he was too busy to be listening to music at home with his kids. The father never got the connection between his lack of modeling at home and his son's lack of interest in classical music. Philanthropy cannot simply be check writing and rhetoric; you have to live your life in a way that models philanthropic involvement.

As children grow, they develop a view of themselves, a view of others, and a view of the world. If you are faced with an adolescent who resists the idea of volunteer work, odds are that you have not been modeling philanthropic involvement when your child was younger. Even if this is the case, you can probably find a way to involve him at this late date. Here are some dos and don'ts to keep in mind as you attempt to involve him:

- Do let your kids know who you are and what values you have by discussing your involvement in philanthropy.
- Do look for a link between your child's interests and a philanthropic activity; attempt to find an endeavor that touches a nerve (e.g., a child who is interested in sports might want to become involved with an organization that helps former athletes down on their luck or that helps young athletes, like the Boys Club).
- Do give your child options if there's no obvious interest-based activity; suggest three or four different types of involvement and see if any interest your child.
- Do be reasonable about your child's time commitment; start out with an activity that only requires his participation once or twice a month (and let him increase his level of participation if he wants to).
- Do participate with your child in the volunteer effort; if she works in a soup kitchen, you should also work in the soup kitchen.
- Do talk with your child about the activity after you participate; give him a chance to express his feelings about what he experienced (most kids have very strong reactions to working with people and in places very different from what they're accustomed to).
- Don't insist she become involved because "you never think of anyone but yourself"; don't try and browbeat her into doing volunteer work.
- Don't make him feel guilty by talking about how much he has and how little others possess. The cookie exercise in Chapter 7 was designed to raise your child's awareness of socioeconomic diversity, not to make him feel guilty.
- Don't lecture her about the importance of philanthropy to society. She may be too young. An adolescent may be going through a completely normal phase of being self-centered.

Don't push. Continue your own involvement in philanthropy
and, from time to time, mention what you are doing.

- Don't turn it into a punishment by saying, "You have to do
this until you show more compassion for others."
- Do take a look at the Appendix for a list of useful Internet
resources.

SILVER NUGGET

Create a list of all the philanthropic organizations you've
given money to in recent years. Which one do you
think would present the greatest opportunity for family
involvement in volunteer activities?

Selecting Opportunities for Involvement

Some parents we've worked with feel intimidated by the sheer
number of charities out there. In 1998 in America there were
more than 47,000 charitable organizations; they gave away an estimated $22 billion in grants and controlled aggregate assets of $385
billion. If there's no clear group that dovetails with your family's
interests—and if you know little about charitable organizations—
you may find it difficult to know how to proceed. To avoid that
possibility, let's define the three basic types of philanthropic
organizations:

1. Public charities
2. Family foundations
3. Community foundations

Philanthropic organizations that receive at least one-third of their operating income from the general public are classified as a public charity by the Internal Revenue Service. An organization supported entirely by one individual or one family is known as a *family foundation* (often known as a *private foundation*). What's the difference? You get to deduct a larger percentage of contributions to public charities than to family foundations. But family foundations are more flexible and allow you to create a philanthropic organization of your own. Community foundations are a blend; they offer the increased tax deduction available for gifts to public charities while providing much of the flexibility of a family foundation.

Let's look at the three broad types of philanthropic organizations in more detail and see how they lend themselves to involving you and your family in philanthropy.

Public Charities

Public charities fall into two basic categories: what we call "traditional charities" and "social-change foundations." Traditional charities tend to focus on long-standing, traditional goals, such as funding medical research, supporting education, or alleviating such symptoms of poverty as hunger or homelessness.

Opportunities abound for involvement with traditional charities, whether it is making contributions or donating time. In fact, many of the largest traditional charities could not function without substantial numbers of volunteers. In 2000 volunteers made up 97 percent of the American Red Cross's total work force and were responsible for activities that ranged from collecting half the nation's entire blood supply to providing emergency assistance to the 150 families forced from their homes by fire every day somewhere in America. Similarly, the Salvation Army relies on volunteers for almost all of its activities, including ringing bells, working in the kitchens, and serving as members of advisory organizations. You will find that most hospitals, retirement homes, assisted-living facilities, and museums welcome volunteers.

JONAH'S STORY

Jonah is a nineteen-year-old who is studying neuroscience at a college in New York. He grew up in Los Angeles in a family in which his father was involved with nonprofits and "a huge part of our life was helping people."

As a sophomore in a Los Angeles public high school, Jonah was looking for a concrete way to get involved. One weekend a friend invited him to work on a Habitat for Humanity house. He spent the day raising walls, hammering nails, and tarring a roof. "I was just blown away by being able to work with the people I was helping."

Jonah was so inspired by his experience that, during his remaining three years in high school, he helped organize a consortium of kids from ten local high schools—five public and five private—who raised more than $300,000 and built five Habitat homes. (It costs roughly $68,000 to build a Habitat home in Los Angeles County.) Every weekend there would be kids from the most affluent neighborhoods in L.A. hammering and cutting, and at the end of the day they could look up and see what they had done with their own hands to help others.

Habitat for Humanity is a nondenominational organization that is dedicated to "building simple, decent, affordable, houses in partnership with those in need of adequate shelter." Contributions from interested individuals and groups provide the funding, and volunteer labor provides the muscle. If you've never lifted a hammer before in your life, Habitat will train you. Houses are built by the homeowner and volunteers under trained supervision and then sold to the homeowner at no profit and at a zero-interest-rate mortgage. Since 1976, volunteers have helped Habitat build more than 100,000 houses in more than sixty countries, including more than 30,000 houses across the United States. Volunteers come from all walks of life and all age groups.

If your child's interests run more toward inside than outside activities, you might consider getting involved in a mentoring program like the Fulfillment Fund in Los Angeles. The fund originated in 1973 when a doctor at the UCLA Medical Center suggested that instead of holding the annual year-end holiday party for the medical staff, they spend the money instead on a party for the physically disabled children at the Medical Center who were unable to spend the holidays at home with their families. By 1977 the party had become an annual event, and the Fulfillment Fund was incorporated as a public charity helping disabled children rise above their disabilities. In a few years the program expanded to include able-bodied students who were recognized by their teachers as having considerable potential that they were unlikely to realize without additional community support. Today the Fulfillment Fund is the largest private donor of scholarship and mentoring assistance in Los Angeles. It does so through a combination of programs, including a college counseling and scholarship program and one-on-one mentoring in which high school students are matched with adults who volunteer to stay in touch throughout the year.

Other opportunities exist for volunteers to participate in after-school enrichment programs. In Los Angeles, Carla Sanger heads L.A.'s BEST (www.lasbest.org), which has become a national model for such programs. Several independent evaluations conducted by the UCLA Center for the Study of Evaluation revealed that children participating in L.A.'s BEST demonstrated higher school attendance and improved performance on standardized tests in mathematics, reading, and language arts in middle and high school.

Or you might consider your neighborhood library, which is yet another underfunded institution that puts volunteers of all age to excellent use. *Creating the Full-Service Homework Center in Your Library* by Cindy Mediavilla, Ph.D., of the department of information studies at UCLA, is a how-to-do-it manual that contains all the information you need to help your local library to set up a successful homework center that gives kids a leg up and a place to go after school.

If your local community does not have mentor programs or homework centers, you and your child could help create one. Although this is an ambitious undertaking, it also meets the needs of children and adults who have an entrepreneurial bent.

Social-change foundations are a form of public charity that usually operate at the grassroots community level in an attempt to catalyze social change. In fact, the Funding Exchange, a national network of fifteen social-change foundations, has the slogan "Philanthropy Committed to Change, Not Charity" to highlight their belief in the necessity of systemic change at the grassroots level. Their boards typically include community activists, people of color, women, poor and working-class people, gays and lesbians, low-income advocates, and people with disabilities. Because social-change foundations specialize in providing small grants—ranging from $500 to $20,000—to grassroots organizations in the local community, they are strategically placed to match volunteers with activist organizations.

Let's look at some representative social-change foundations that are looking for volunteers. The following are some representative member foundations listed on the Funding Exchange's website, www.fex.org:

• In Los Angeles, Liberty Hill Foundation, founded in 1976 by four philanthropists, including heiress and movie producer Sarah Pillsbury, offers start-up grants to grassroots community organizations and conducts programs that expose affluent Westside families to the realities of life on the other side of the city's socioeconomic divide. Four times a year, Liberty Hill provides Saturday van tours for teenagers interested in environmental problems in Los Angeles, with stops at major cleanup sites and explanations of the environmental problems facing that particular community.

• In New York City, the North Star Fund, named after an antislavery newspaper started by Frederick Douglass in 1847, supports such community organizations as Deep Dish TV, the first and only grassroots television network in the United States, and Mothers on the Move, Inc., a grassroots membership organization located in the Hunts Point/Longwood/Port Morris sections of the South Bronx, which has successfully conducted an adult literacy program, won increased regulation of the numerous waste transfer stations in the Hunts Point area, and conducted a community action program that led the Department of Parks and Recreation to set aside $900,000 to rehabilitate abandoned tennis courts into a community-designed multiuse park.

• The Fund for Southern Communities in Decatur, Georgia, provides funding for community action programs in Georgia, North Carolina, and South Carolina. In Georgia, the fund works with a group of nine- to nineteen-year-olds that uses dance, music, and theater to educate their peers about drugs, AIDS, gang violence, and date rape; in South Carolina, it helps fund an African American–led group that organizes and empowers women and youth in a poor rural area to address issues such as environmental abuse and racism within the judicial system.

Family Foundations

If you really want to involve the children in philanthropy, you should know about family foundations (also known as private foundations). They are philanthropic organizations created and controlled by a single family. Several types exist, but the most common form is the conduit, or nonoperating, foundation. This type of foundation does not directly engage in philanthropic activities. Instead, it makes grants to other organizations that do, such as the Salvation Army or Red Cross. Federal law requires family foundations to make grants each year equal to at least 5 percent of their assets. There are about 40,000 family foundations in America today. They range in size from "mom and pop" foundations, with less than $25,000, to the Bill and Melinda Gates Foundation, with an endowment of more than $20 billion.

Alan Alda spoke about his experiences with a family foundation during the Council on Foundations' 1995 Family Foundation Conference.

> First of all, why we did it. For one thing, we wanted to involve our children in giving. From the time we taught our children how to wash their hands, whenever we wanted them to know something, we didn't just tell them about it, we did it with them. We'd put their hands between ours, stick them under the faucet and rub. And that's what we've done with philanthropy.
>
> From the beginning, we've been on an equal footing with them. Everyone has an equal vote. Arlene and I as founders

don't have any greater influence just because we gave the money in the first place. We don't even have any moral advantage in an argument. It's maddeningly democratic. One person, one damn vote.

(The full text of Alda's inspiring speech is posted at the website of the Philanthropic Initiative, www.tpi.org.)

There is a wealth of resources available if you decide to create and run a family foundation. A first step might be to purchase the writing and speeches of Paul Ylvisaker, collected in Virginia M. Esposito's *Conscience and Community: The Legacy of Paul Ylvisaker.* Ylvisaker is viewed by many as the intellectual and philosophical conscience of modern philanthropy in America. Ylvisaker taught at Harvard, Yale, Princeton, and Swarthmore; served as chairman of the Task Force on the Cities under President Lyndon B. Johnson; was director of the Public Policy Program at the Ford Foundation; and was the first commissioner of Community Affairs for the state of New Jersey. Ylvisaker cautioned us not to assume that having money with which to help others is the same as having answers as to how best to deliver that help.

A definite second step—and your first step if you are more interested in the nuts and bolts of philanthropy than in its philosophical basis—is contacting the Council on Foundations, a nonprofit membership organization of grant-making public and private foundations. Start by acquiring *A Founder's Guide to the Family Foundation: How to Use, Govern, and Enjoy Your Family Foundation.* This is a short (thirty-four-page) overview of most of the critical issues involved in the family foundation, including foundation governance, gift requests, grant-making, board responsibilities, and roles of the founder. If you decide to proceed, purchase the Family Foundation Library series, which consists of four booklets covering family dynamics, the ABCs of governing a family foundation, the grant-making process, and grant management.

Community Foundations

For some families, a community foundation offers many of the advantages of the family foundation without the costs involved. Community foundations are a specialized form of public charity that are the brainchild of Cleveland, Ohio, banker Frederick Goff. In 1914 Goff became concerned by the large number of charitable bequests that his bank's trust department was managing. Goff felt that many of those bequests were so inflexible that they could not meet the constantly changing needs of the community. He was also concerned that the administrative fees involved in managing the separate bequests were eating into principal and dissipating the funds. Goff's solution was the community foundation. His bank would combine all of the charitable bequests into a single managed account, thereby substantially lowering the administrative costs, and would turn over responsibility for distributing the income to a separate entity—the Cleveland Foundation—a publicly appointed, volunteer board of leading citizens with the flexibility to respond to the changing needs of the community. Today, there are about 450 community foundations in the United States.

For many families, community foundations offer all of the advantages and none of the disadvantages of private foundations. To understand how a community foundation operates, let's look at the California Community Foundation (CCF). CCF was established in Los Angeles in 1915. It has a current endowment of $525 million and plans to make grants during 2001 of more than $110 million. Like many community foundations, CCF offers donors

SILVER NUGGET

Talk to friends and neighbors, as well as clergy and members of your church, synagogue, or mosque, about their involvement with public charities and foundations; these discussions will probably yield a number of options for you and your family.

the opportunity to create a "Donor Advised Fund" as an alternative to a family foundation. In a Donor Advised Fund, you make a tax-deductible contribution to CCF, which invests the contribution as part of its general assets. Because CCF is treated as a public charity, you are likely to get a larger charitable deduction than if you had made the same contribution to your own family foundation. A separate fund is created within CCF in your name or your family's name. Although you are not involved in investing the funds contributed to CCF, you retain the ability to recommend organizations and programs you'd like to support. You may get your kids involved in selecting the appropriate charitable recipients in exactly the same manner as if you had created a family foundation. CCF will review your recommendations to ensure that the organizations or programs qualify as charitable and meet the basic guidelines it has established. If so, a check in your name is sent to the organization. Because CCF is a public charity, a Donor Advised Fund is exempt from the requirement that it distribute not less than 5 percent annually. As a result, you have the flexibility of being able to accumulate funds for several years, to increase the underlying asset value of your fund.

Putting Your Philanthropy Plan into Action

Now that you're aware of the various types of philanthropic possibilities, you need to get the process rolling. Although there are all sorts of ways to do this, we've found that the following steps provide a good guide for moving forward.

Integrate Philanthropic Giving and Volunteerism into Conversation

Your philanthropic ideas shouldn't come out of left field. If your child feels that your request that he participate in a philanthropic endeavor is calculated or suggests a hidden agenda, he'll probably resist. Therefore, when you and your spouse make a donation to a charity, mention it at the dinner table and explain why you support that organization. If you volunteer, briefly describe what you did. Don't make a big deal of it. Instead, the goal is to make the topic familiar to your children at an early age and allow your children to get to know who you are and what your values are by sharing with them what you do.

Be Alert for Teachable Moments

At some point, your child is going to ask you a question about a charity you've mentioned or your volunteer work. Some parents don't take their child's questions seriously and give them a quick, uninformative answer. At the other extreme, they deliver a boring lecture about the obligation for every citizen to do good works. What you should do is treat the question seriously and respond with a concise but informative answer. A younger child may seem to be asking a silly question, such as, "Why do you want to save the whales, anyway?" or he may only make a statement, "Homeless people sure are important to you." This is your opening to communicate that philanthropy is a family value. Your response can be a simple as, "I really feel bad for people who don't have a home, and I want to do something that can make their lives a little easier."

Create a "Virtual Foundation" and a "Family Giving Pool"

If you don't want to establish a private foundation, why not establish a "virtual foundation" and let your children participate. Stan and Karen budgeted $100 for their ten-year-old son, Harry, to give away during the year. They helped him identify charities and foundations that dealt with Harry's interests: the environment, endangered animals, and children with medical problems. Every three months, Harry could give away $25. At dinner, Harry would explain which organizations he wanted to give money to and his reasons for choosing those particular organizations. Stan and Karen would write the checks, but Harry would write a short cover note and mail the contributions. Giving Harry the ability to select the recipients and participate in the process of giving encouraged him to think and talk about a variety of social issues. As a result, Harry was more aware of these issues than other children his age. He was also learning how his family's affluence could be used in socially responsible ways.

Joe and Clarice adopted a similar concept. Starting when their children were twelve and fourteen, Joe and Clarice would save all the philanthropic solicitations they received in the mail. At the end of each month, they would lay them out on a table for everyone to read, pointing out any solicitations that appeared suspicious or failed to provide adequate information about how donations would be used. Joe and Clarice would explain how much money was in the "family giving pool" that month—the amount available for philanthropy. If money was tight one month, the pool might be relatively small. In a good month, it would be larger.

There would then be a family vote on which charities to support. Everyone had a vote. If there was a deadlock, with the votes equally divided, they used a concept known as "Council," a technique introduced by Brent W. Kessel, the President of Abacus Wealth Management, Inc., in Santa Monica, California. In various forms, Council is used by nonprofits and major corporations throughout America. The basic concepts are simple:

- Sit in a circle so that no one is at the head of the table.

- Establish a "talking piece." It can range from a family heirloom to a toy. Only the person holding the talking piece can speak. Interrupting is forbidden.

- Really listen. Most of the time we listen to someone only long enough to prepare our response, and family members are notorious for interrupting each other. In Council you really have to listen to what the other person is saying, even if it's your youngest child.

- When it's your turn to speak, explain your choice. Don't ramble. Get to the heart of the matter. And be spontaneous. If you are really listening to what everyone else is saying, you will be talking from your heart rather than trying to make a debate point. Almost always, Council is able to break a deadlock.

Capitalize on Your Child's Interest

When your kids express interest in a particular charity's work, capitalize on that interest by exploring how you and your children might become actively involved. Call up the charity and ask if they have any existing volunteer programs designed specifically for children and their parents. If they don't usually use children as volunteers, you might ask if they can think of a task that would be well suited to someone your child's age. Once you find something suitable, mention the possibility to your child and see how he reacts. If he's enthusiastic, give it a shot. Ask him to make a commitment of his time (perhaps one hour per week) for a few months. You would be surprised at the opportunities that exist. Andy was interested in dogs. His parents introduced him to Create-a-Smile, a program sponsored by International Wildlife Education and Conservation, which involves taking specially trained dogs to visit with autistic children, hospitalized patients, the elderly, and others.

Here are a few guidelines that will help make your child's activity a rewarding experience:

• **Participate with your child.** Don't just drop her off at the door and pick her up an hour later. Model the type of behavior you want her to adopt by working side by side.

• **Talk about the activity.** Your joint volunteer efforts aren't just something you do but something you discuss. Most kids have a million questions about the new people they meet and the environment in which they do their volunteer service; they're especially fascinated if they're working in a poor neighborhood or with people who *appear* different from the ones they usually interact with. These are great opportunities to have rich discussions about people who are struggling. Why are poor people poor? Why does someone not have a home? Why did someone in a shelter talk in that "funny" way? Why do some adults need help in learning how to read? Why is the river that we're trying to clean polluted? These and other questions are the start of experiences that are valuable to all children but especially those who might otherwise be sheltered from the diversity of the world.

• **Switch activities when appropriate.** Kids' interests change, and you need to recognize that they may grow out of a particular volunteer activity. What might have excited them when they were ten may not be as relevant when they're thirteen. For this reason, be alert for new volunteer opportunities that might be better suited to their age and interests. They may develop a sudden passion for ecology as adolescents or find themselves drawn to helping Spanish-speaking immigrants when they become semifluent in the language in school. Let your child's changing interests lead to new volunteer efforts rather than imposing your interests upon him.

Neutral Ground

Finally, philanthropy provides you with the chance to talk about money without a lot of the emotional baggage that's often attached to the subject. Most of the time, money discussions with children occur in the context of "our money" or "your money." Either we're explaining how we use or manage our money or the conversation is about our children's use or management of their allowance or the money they are earning from a part-time job. No matter how hard we try to stop it, lecturing and displaying emotions often sneak into the conversation. It's easy for arguments to erupt and for the point of a discussion to get lost.

Philanthropy takes a lot of emotion out of money discussions. You can talk about money issues without lecturing your children about responsibility and fiscal prudence, and your kids can talk without feeling deprived or guilty. When the goal of money is primarily to help others, children can feel more comfortable with financial discussions and really listen to what you have to say about the subject. It's another opportunity to share your thoughts, ideas, and beliefs with one another.

Family Wealth Planning

L ike allowances and philanthropy, estate planning is part of family wealth management and needs to be connected to your values. Complicating matters, transferring money to your children and grandchildren involves significant psychological and emotional issues. We're going to look at how this transfer can be a positive rather than a negative child-raising experience.

At first glance, an estate plan may seem secondary or even irrelevant to your goal of raising an emotionally healthy child. You may believe that such a plan deals with an event that won't happen for many years and thus won't affect your child during the crucial developmental stages. In fact, handled properly, estate planning can have a profoundly positive influence on your children in many ways. Estate planning provides a great forum for discussing financial issues with your kids. The seriousness of the subject—their future, your possible absence from their lives—helps them really think about what money means to them. On the other hand, estate planning designed solely to save taxes and detached from your values can sabotage efforts to raise responsible children. A classic example of this problem is posed by parents who have taken advantage of their ability to give $20,000 tax free to their child each year, but who are opposed to giving large unrestricted sums of money to their children when they are young. Many parents simply open a custodial account for their child at their local bank and add $20,000 to that account each year. These parents don't realize that a child is legally entitled to the money in a custodial account at age eighteen, by which time interest would have increased the account to more than $500,000. Suppose the parents intended to pay for their child's college tuition and room and board but wanted the child to get a part-time job to pay for gas and entertainment. The child's response may well be that there is no need for a part-time job when he is receiving more than $2,000 a month in interest income from the account. The parents should have consulted an estate-planning specialist who could have helped them create a trust that reflected their values. For example, the trust could have provided that the funds stay in trust until the child attains age twenty-five or graduates from college, at which time the funds would be available to help the child go into business or buy a home. Only after you have decided on how to transfer family wealth in a manner consistent with your values can you begin to integrate these goals with whatever tax-saving techniques you might adopt.

SILVER NUGGET

Talk with your spouse about how your child might react if you were to tell her that you planned to give her *X* number of dollars on her twenty-first birthday.

The Nuts and Bolts

We've had some kind of estate tax since 1797. A tax bill signed by President George W. Bush in June 2001 provides for the phase out of the estate tax by 2010. But, in a scenario right out of *Alice in Wonderland*, that same tax bill reenacts the estate tax in 2011! As a result, we'll be dealing with the estate tax for some time to come. And some estate-planning concepts—like the use of trusts—will be very important even without an estate tax.

Before talking to your kids (or a lawyer, for that matter) about an estate plan, you should have a grasp of what's involved. In this way you'll be better prepared to integrate your values into whatever strategy you choose.

Most advisors will recommend that you make lifetime gifts to your children and grandchildren. Under the current tax system, it is cheaper to pay gift taxes than estate taxes. To understand why this is so, we need to understand the difference between a *tax-inclusive* and a *tax-exclusive* system. In a tax-inclusive system, everything is taxed, including the dollars you use to pay the tax. The income tax is a good example of a tax-inclusive system. It taxes your entire income, including the dollars that you use to pay the tax. The estate tax is a tax-inclusive system; every dollar in your estate is taxed, including the dollars your heirs use to pay the estate taxes. On the other hand, gift taxes are tax exclusive. The gift tax is imposed only on the property that you give away. The dollars you use to pay the gift tax are not taxed.

Here's an easy way to visualize the important difference between gift taxes and estate taxes. Just for this example, pretend that you are worth $1 million and that the gift tax and estate tax rates are both 50 percent. We also want you to pretend that the entire $1 million will either be subject to gift tax if you give it away now or estate tax if you wait until you die. You want your kids to get as much as possible. If you wait until you die, the estate tax is 50 percent, or $500,000. You have two sets of equal heirs: the government and the kids each get $500,000. If you make a lifetime gift, you have a total of $1 million out of which to make a gift to the kids and pay the gift taxes. If you give the kids

$500,000, which is the same amount they would get at your death, the gift tax will be $250,000 and you'll have $250,000 left. Right away it becomes obvious that the kids can get more from a lifetime gift than by inheriting your estate when you pass away. In fact, your kids keep not just one-half ($500,000) but two-thirds ($667,000) of your assets if you give them away during your lifetime. You might think of lifetime gifts as a good way to partially disinherit the IRS!

Your advisors will also probably recommend that you make those gifts to trusts for your children, rather than giving them the property outright. There are several reasons why people use trusts, and many of them have nothing to do with taxes. If your estate is distributed outright to your children, their inheritance could be attached by their creditors if they are sued. If they ever declare bankruptcy, their inheritance would be subject to the jurisdiction of the bankruptcy court. And in the event of a divorce, your child's ex may be able to convince the judge that your child converted the inheritance into jointly owned property and the ex is entitled to half! On the other hand, property held in a properly drafted trust for your children is exempt from their creditors and the bankruptcy court and is protected from the claims of a child's ex in a divorce proceeding.

If your children are young or inexperienced with money management, you will need to appoint someone to serve as trustee and manage the trust for them. You might select a trusted friend or advisor. Another alternative is to use the trust department of a bank or a trust company. It is also very common for these trusts to give the trustee discretion in determining the appropriate amounts to be distributed to the children.

Keeping this information in mind, let's return to the topic of children and the impact of money on their lives. The previous paragraph gives us a good starting point because, as you read, two questions might have occurred to you:

- Who guides the trustee in determining how money from the trust is distributed?
- How can we make sure that the money is distributed in a way that reflects our values and contributes to the emotional health of our child?

Communicating Values Through an Estate Plan

Jon's office in Century City overlooks the back lot of Twentieth Century Fox. When Jon meets with a new client to discuss estate planning, one of the topics is the role of lifetime gifts in transferring family wealth to children and grandchildren. But rather than talking about the tax savings, he centers the conversation around the clients' values and goals. "Do you remember the movie *Heaven Can Wait*" Jon asks, "in which Warren Beatty gets prematurely called to heaven by an overly eager angel and talks the angel into sending him back to earth in the body of a billionaire? Let's redo *Heaven Can Wait*, but this time with you in the starring role, and we'll have the angels bring you back as the Trustee of a trust for your children which now has all of your assets. The rest of the movie is going to be about how you run that trust. So, for what purposes would you be distributing money to your kids? What would you like to see your children and grandchildren do, and what are you afraid might happen? What might they do with the money that would disappoint you?"

Most of Jon's clients take some time to answer; they may have dealt with other estate planners, but these are questions no one has ever asked them before. And they often have difficulty coming up with answers.

To find the answers, look to your values. In Chapter 4, as part of an exercise (creating a family mission statement), you articulated values that you want your family to emulate. With these values in mind, you can determine how best to structure a program of giving to your children. For example, if education is an important family value, can you structure gifts that will encourage and assist your children and grandchildren in attaining a college and postgraduate education? If entrepreneurship is a family value, can you use gifts to encourage and assist them in starting their own businesses and obtaining the technical and financial skills necessary to make them a success?

We worked with a couple several years ago who placed great value on being self-sufficient and relying on oneself to succeed in the face of adversity. Their initial reaction to lifetime giving was negative. They recognized the tax advantages of lifetime gifts but felt that the negative impact of gifts on self-sufficiency far outweighed the advantages. This couple, however, had a twenty-year-old son who had dropped out of college because classes interfered with surfing. He surfed every morning and supported himself by building surfboards in the afternoon, which he sold to friends and acquaintances. His mother was horrified that he had dropped his classes, and his father, a successful entrepreneur, explained at length (and with some heat) why his son would be unable to support himself: his profit margin was too small; he couldn't make enough boards; he couldn't afford to advertise. The list was endless. Had the son asked for money, we inquired? No. Would he have a good chance of success if he found an investor? Probably, said the father, but no one is dumb enough to invest with a twenty-year-old college dropout. Maybe *you* should consider being that dumb, we suggested.

The parents realized that a gift that saved taxes for the family could also communicate deeply held values to their child. They created a trust for their son and made a gift to it of enough money to form a corporation that would build and market surfboards. Their son would be the CEO of the corporation. Their CPA was the treasurer. When their son was thirty-five, the trust would end and he would become the sole owner of the corporation. It was up to him whether the corporation would be valuable or value-less. In the six years since the corporation was formed, it's grown to five full-time employees, and their son recently enrolled in a night-school business program at a local community college.

The family mission statement has several other uses in the estate-planning process, including the following:

- If you make gifts in trust, the mission statement will help your attorney draft a trust that incorporates your values.
- It allows you to communicate your values to future generations; it passes on your beliefs to descendants you may never have the opportunity to meet.

SILVER NUGGET

Create your own estate plan in simple, nonlawyerly language that incorporates your family mission statement.

When you create a trust fund for your family that is intended to last at least two generations, some of your descendants who will benefit from the trust will likely be born after you pass away. In the absence of the family mission statement, how will they know about your values and what motivated you in creating the trust? In addition, if you incorporate the mission statement in the trust, you are providing the trustee with much-needed general guidance when evaluating requests by beneficiaries for distributions from the trust.

Talking to Your Children About Your Estate Plan

Let's assume that you have put your family mission statement on paper and feel that a lifetime gift is consistent with your values. The next step is to articulate and discuss your concerns about transferring family wealth to your children.

Many of our clients are initially appalled at the concept of talking about their estate plan with their children. It is not at all uncommon for Jon to work with clients in their fifties and sixties who have no idea of their parents' net worth, let alone their estate plan. A study by U.S. Trust, one of the oldest trust companies in America, disclosed that less than one-third of millionaires had shared their estate plan with their adult children.

John Levy, a pioneer researcher on the effects of money on children and an advisor to wealthy families in Northern California, observes that not only is it common not to share estate plans with children but "when kids work up the courage to ask their parents for specifics, they often get slapped down."

Perhaps the single most common reason we hear from our clients for why they don't want to share their estate plan (and their net worth) with their children is that "knowing how much we have and what they are going to inherit will harm them. It will demotivate them." Levy points out that if you look at this concern, you will see that it is built on two underlying concepts. The first is, "making a lot of money is the most important thing for my child to do. I don't want to do anything that interferes with this goal; if my child knows she has a trust fund or that I'm worth a lot of money, she may not work hard or may select a job that doesn't produce a high income." Second, "I'm raising a child who lacks both a work ethic and a sense of responsibility." Our reply is that making a lot of money might be important for some people, but for others money may be far less important than becoming a writer, artist, or teacher or being involved in philanthropy. The world needs poets as well as successful entrepreneurs. Affluence, handled properly, makes it possible for your child to become either. If you raise your child with a strong work ethic and a sense of responsibility, she will want to do the best she can do no matter what career path is taken or how much is in the trust fund.

On the other hand, several prominent estate planners with whom we have discussed these matters agree that if you have raised children who lack both a work ethic and a sense of responsibility, you should think twice before telling them how much they are going to inherit because doing so will do nothing more than increase their sense of entitlement. If you find yourself in this situation, you really have more important issues to worry about than whether to discuss your estate plan with your adult Peter Pan.

Do trust funds really demotivate kids? Many of the most wealthy American families have created trusts for their children, but they have also worried about creating too large a trust fund. "The parent who leaves his son enormous wealth," Andrew Carnegie wrote in an 1891 essay, "generally deadens the talents and energies of the son and tempts him to lead a less useful and less worthy life than he otherwise would." Warren E. Buffett, the richest man in America until he was unseated by Bill Gates, was quoted in the 1990s as saying that he was in favor of giving his children enough money that they can do anything but not so much that they could do nothing. Other families, such as the Waltons of WalMart fame, have done exactly the opposite, leaving vast fortunes to their children. It hasn't seemed to harm some of them, at least from what is reported about them in the news. Sam Walton's oldest son, S. Robson Walton, worth $20 billion or so (some of which is through trust funds), is a Columbia Law School graduate, an Iron Man triathlete, and chairman of the board of the world's largest retailer. He may have other issues in his life, but he certainly does not seem demotivated.

Based on our observation of clients, friends, and family and our reading of the literature, we believe that trust funds actually seem to serve as an incentive for children who are entrepreneurial but might be a disincentive for children who work as employees. In a study published in the 1994 *Journal of Political Economy*, Douglas Holtz-Eakin, David Joulfaian, and Harvey S. Rosen determined that entrepreneurs who received significant inheritances from their parents were more likely to stay in business for themselves than entrepreneurs who did not receive significant inheritances. Moreover, the revenues of companies run by the entrepreneurs who received larger inheritances grew 20 percent faster. On the other hand, a study by the same authors in the May 1993 *Quarterly Journal of Economics* of the tax returns of 2,500 Americans who received inheritances in 1982 concluded that the more money you leave your children, the more likely they are to retire. "A single person who receives an inheritance of about $150,000 is four times more likely to leave the labor force than a person with an inheritance below $25,000." The problem with this conclusion is that the study was conducted under such strict safeguards to protect the anonymity of the taxpayers that we know nothing at all about the inheritors except how much they received. Based on our experience with inheritance patterns, it seems likely that the people receiving the larger gifts were probably older children who might have been approaching retirement age, and those receiving smaller bequests were probably younger children or grandchildren and thus less likely to retire.

If you decide to create a trust for your children, or if your parents or grandparents have already done so, Judy Barber, a family business consultant in San Francisco, stresses the need to help your children develop a guiding passion in life. It may involve philanthropy. It may be entrepreneurship or becoming an architect, a teacher, or a musician. Freud has observed that each of us has two major needs in life: to be loved by another and to feel competent. If our children are economically secure and can maintain at least a middle-class lifestyle without working, they need to develop a purpose that helps guide their lives. If they have such a guiding interest, we have found that the trust fund is not a disincentive to responsible behavior. Without a guiding interest, problems can occur. As the mother of three adult children who began receiving distributions from their grandfather's trust at age eighteen has observed, a trust fund enables children to live a "half life" in which they neither have to work nor have a guiding interest that gives meaning to their lives. Instead, the trust distributions might simply "buffer them from harsh reality." One of her children found himself in agreement. In our interview with him, he commented that he wished he had not received the money at such a young age because it created problems of self-worth. Although society expected him to work, he didn't have to. Although it gave him the room to explore different lifestyles, too much money too early made it "tough to gain a sense of the value of money and easier to burn through it."

If you have concerns about the effect of creating a trust for your children, talk to them about your concerns. You might be surprised at their reaction. The adult son of one of our clients recently asked his parents not to make a significant gift. "I'm a hunter and gatherer right now," he said. "I'm learning how to handle it and make things work. I don't want you to put a bunch of berries in front of me that I didn't find on my own. That would defeat the purpose." Expect a range of reactions from your kids when you start talking about gifts and trusts. Some children are surprised by the amount that you intend to leave them. Many kids are worried about their ability to manage the money, and others are concerned that they will prove unworthy of the gift. The more you talk about both their concerns and your own, the more you can communicate and reinforce your underlying values.

Another issue you need to discuss with the children is whether there are conditions on the gifts you make to them. Even if there are no express conditions, there may be expectations that you need to articulate. You may have expectations about how the children will show gratitude for your largesse. If you give your son and his wife $50,000 for the down payment on a house, do you expect to be invited over to the new house for dinner regularly? Do you expect them to buy a house in a certain price range? Do you expect them to look for a house in your area? You may also harbor expectations about how they will manage the money and end up judging their every expense. For instance, how would you feel if you gave your daughter a $10,000 gift to help her defray educational expenses and learned she used $2,000 of it to take a vacation?

Therefore, identify your own expectations and then tell your children what you expect. Don't give them a gift and feel that it's unmannerly to attach conditions to it. If you have expectations or want to attach conditions, be specific. Being specific not only helps avoid conflicts in the future, but it also gives your child the opportunity to decline the gift if the conditions are unacceptable. Don't be vague or wishy-washy about what you hope they'll use the money for: "Here's $10,000, and though you can use it however you want, it might be a good idea if you put it toward something useful." It's far better to say: "I've decided to give you $10,000 so that you can buy stocks and learn about investing." Or: "We know you're strapped for time with your schedule, so we want you to buy a car to get you to and from your various activities. We're going to give you $10,000 so you can buy a safe used car."

Keeping in mind that every family is unique, here are our suggestions about talking to your children about your estate plan.

Young Children

If a child under age eighteen or so raises the subject, you have a wonderful opportunity for a conversation. Levy cautions us to treat such questions from young children about the estate plan as an appropriate topic for them to raise. Don't make them feel wrong for bringing up the subject. Respond to their questions on a level that they can understand, and try to grasp why they are asking the questions.

It's been our experience that younger children tend to bring up the topic of wills and trusts under the following circumstances:

• Your child may be filled with anxiety because she came across a draft of a will or trust that was left lying around in the living room or she overheard a comment that you made, often to your spouse, about the estate plan. She may be convinced that you are terminally ill. In this situation you need to reassure your child that signing a will doesn't mean you are planning on dying soon. Explain that people have wills simply as a precaution, just like you have insurance on your house or car.

• Your child may be seeking reassurance that you don't love his siblings more than him. When eleven-year-old Johnny asks if you are providing for him in your will, an appropriate answer is that you are taking care of all of your children equally.

• Your child may want reassurance that she is safe. She may have heard about a will contest on TV or the parent of a friend or schoolmate might have died. When she asks about your will, she may really be asking whether she will be OK if something happens to you.

• Finally, your child may have talked about wills and trusts with a friend or schoolmate and is curious. Perhaps a friend will receive money at age eighteen from a trust that was established by his parents or grandparents and your child may assume that this happens to everyone. Talk to him about the type of financial assistance you are planning to provide when he (and his siblings) reach a given age.

Adult Children

We recommend that you use your estate plan as another opportunity to talk about money and responsibility with your adult children. Most affluent parents do not intend to support their adult children. Although they may intend to assist them from time to time through annual gifts or possibly with such major purchases as a home, they want their children to live responsible and self-supporting lives. If the bulk of the family wealth is going to pass to the children only after you pass away, discussing your estate plan with them helps them understand what they're going to receive and when, allowing them to plan their lives accordingly. This approach works best in families that began educating their kids about money when they were young, and the children already possess some knowledge of the family's net worth.

Eric and Monica took advantage of a wisecrack by one of their adult children during a family vacation at an exclusive resort to talk about how they were going to divide their assets among the children. When one of the children observed that the vacation was so nice that he was afraid that his parents were "spending my inheritance," Monica responded that they were spending their own money, not the kids'. In fact, Monica told them, she and Eric had decided to leave each child a significant sum as their inheritance but to give the bulk of their estate to a private foundation they were going to create. One of the children, who was still in college, was impressed by her parent's desire to help others and said, "Think of how much good can be done with that money!" She asked who was going to run the foundation, and when her parents replied that they had not yet decided, the child expressed interest in working with the foundation when she graduated.

We believe that talking to the children about your estate plan is particularly necessary if you intend to treat children differently. An estate-planning lawyer with many years of experience once observed to us that discovering only after your parents die that they have treated you differently from your siblings can be a rude shock that results in an irreparable breach among family members. He recommended that parents hold a family meeting in which they explain in their own words why they are treating their children differently.

Every estate-planning lawyer, however, has some clients who impulsively change their estate plans whenever there is a family dispute. If they have a disagreement with a child, their first step is to change their will and reduce the child's share of the estate. Several months later, when things have calmed down, they usually tell the lawyer to revise the will again so that everyone is treated equally. If you are one of these people, we strongly recommend against convening family meetings to announce who is in and who is out of the will this week. We find that such an approach tends to be highly destructive and should be avoided.

Some estate-planning techniques involve forming various partnerships or trusts involving different children. A family meeting in which these techniques are discussed and explained can keep some members of the family from jumping to the wrong conclusions. Jon has been consulted on several occasions by individuals convinced that one or more siblings were engaged in a nefarious plot to seize control of the family wealth only to discover that the "plot" was part of a sophisticated estate plan that had not been properly explained to the children.

Incentivizing Values-Based Behavior

An *incentive-based estate plan* is essentially a discretionary trust that attempts to encourage responsible behavior and discourage a trust-fund-kid mentality. Rather than simply relying on the trustee to exercise discretion consistent with your family mission statement, an incentive-based plan offers concrete examples of specific types of behavior that you wish to encourage.

You should understand that incentive trust arrangements need not be restricted to trusts that are created by your will when you pass away. Most sophisticated family wealth planning techniques involve lifetime gifts to complicated trust arrangements commonly referred to by their initials, such as a GRAT (Grantor Retained Annuity Trust), GRUT (Grantor Retained Unitrust), or QPRT (Qualified Personal Residence Trust). These trusts can also employ incentive provisions for your children. Because these trusts are created while you are alive, as opposed to trusts created by your will, they offer a marvelous opportunity for you to see how your children respond to the incentive provisions and use the money they receive.

These incentives aren't magical. If you've ignored communicating the values and modeling the money behaviors we've discussed throughout this book, no estate planner can draft anything that will fix everything. On the other hand, incentives can reinforce the values you've been stressing. Creating these incentives is a great exercise in that it forces parents to sit down and think long and hard about what types of behaviors (and underlying values) they want their children to exhibit. Just as importantly, they communicate these behavioral goals to kids in advance of the time they need to exhibit them. Thus, it gives them something to think about and work toward.

The Appendix contains typical incentive provisions that Jon often uses for clients who have young children, as well as an example of an incentive trust that provides the trustee with a great deal of discretion.

Incentives can run the gamut, and you certainly aren't limited by the two examples in the Appendix. For instance, Charles and

Allison decided on a different type of approach. They valued hard work and philanthropy and didn't want their children to become reliant on trust funds. At the same time, they wanted their children to have the option of making philanthropic endeavors their lives' work, knowing that this was an area that interested them. Jon helped them create trusts where all of the income was to be reinvested until each child reached age fifty, at which time the child would start receiving the income. If a child decided to make philanthropy her career, however, she would be entitled to receive income from the trust on a current basis to help provide for her support. In this manner, Charles and Allison incentivized philanthropic careers but also allowed for the possibility that their children would choose nonphilanthropic paths. In the latter case, they wanted to be sure that they maintained a strong work ethic, and the plan helped point their children in this direction.

Trusts as Tools to Teach Money Management

All of us have read stories about people who received millions of dollars from trusts and squandered their newfound wealth in short order. These stories almost always involve situations where a large sum of money is suddenly dumped on someone with no knowledge or training in money management. Some kids growing up in affluent homes have the notion that money grows on trees, that they have so much that they'll never run out of it, and, if they do, they can magically grow some more. As a result, they are incapable of exercising restraint when they receive the money from a trust. The biggest error parents commit when creating trusts is failing to structure them in such a manner that they provide an opportunity for their children to learn money management.

Psychologically, trusts are meaningful to your kids in ways that other money subjects aren't. After all, it's *their* money that's in trust, and a fifteen-year-old is likely to pay much more attention to a discussion of *his* trust than he is to a "drier" discussion of investments.

We have four suggestions that will help you turn a trust into an educational money management vehicle long before your kids actually start receiving trust monies. To make those suggestions work, however, it helps to have two different trustees who are responsible for the administrative and distributive functions. For the distributive trustee, you might want to enlist a family member or friend who you feel will follow your family mission statement in deciding when and in what amounts distributions should be made. The administrative trustee is usually a financial advisor in a bank trust department or professional trust company, and his function is limited to management of trust assets.

Now let's look at the four things you can do to maximize the educational value of your trust:

1. The trust agreement (the document that creates the trust) should provide that all children who have reached age fifteen are to meet at least once a year with the administrative trustee. At the meeting, the administrative trustee will explain both how and why the assets of the trust are currently invested. This gives the administrative trustee the opportunity to introduce your children to concepts such as asset allocation and investing for growth or income.

2. At some point your child should become a coadministrative trustee of her trust. You need to select an age for this purpose, such as when the child reaches age eighteen, twenty-one, or twenty-five. You might also want to key it to an event, such as when your child completes two classes in investing or when she graduates from college. Your child is now involved in day-to-day management of her own trust and is getting a hands-on education in her coadministrative capacity.

3. After several years of serving as a coadministrative trustee, your child should "graduate" to sole administrative trustee and assume responsibility for trust management and investment. A properly drafted trust agreement will allow the administrative trustee to hire money managers to assist in investing trust assets. Again, this will serve as a kind of postgraduate course in money management.

4. You may want to structure the trust so that your child becomes the sole distributive trustee at some age. If you do this, your child is now able to exercise complete control over his trust. By doing so, you're essentially communicating to him that you feel he is sufficiently responsible to handle his trust without any help or limitations. Remember, however, that by continuing to keep the property in trust rather than distributing it outright, you are providing your child with important protection from lawsuits, bankruptcy, and divorce.

Use Your Estate Plan to Link Family Wealth Planning to Philanthropy

By making philanthropy an integral element of your estate plan, you don't just incentivize future philanthropic involvement, but you communicate how much you value such involvement now. You want to get this message across to your children frequently and in various ways. By doing so, you can counter the effect of living in an affluent area where your child's friends may ignore the problems of less-affluent members of society and influence your child to do likewise. Kids are less likely to be negatively impacted by the money all around them if they develop a healthy perspective about and involvement in philanthropic works. To that end, consider the following three techniques.

Teach Your Children to Tithe

As part of the trust fund you establish, stipulate that a designated percentage of the trust's income—often 5 percent to 10 percent— is to be distributed each year to one or more charitable or philanthropic organizations selected by the child. The trustee is often authorized to use trust funds to assist the child in selecting charities, such as retaining a consultant to help identify charities working in areas of interest to the child.

Use the Jackie Method

Jacqueline Kennedy Onassis employed a family philanthropy planning technique known as a charitable income trust to save estate taxes and involve her children in philanthropy. A *charitable income trust* is an irrevocable trust to which you contribute income-producing property. The trust provides that it will pay an annuity (a fixed sum of money) to one or more charities for a number of years. When this period expires, the trust is administered for your children. When you create the trust, you specify how much is to be distributed to charity each year and for how many years these distributions will continue. You also provide what happens to the trust once it is no longer making distributions to charity. For example, Jackie's will provided that a committee composed of her two children; her attorney, Alexander Forger; and her companion, Maurice Tempelsman, were to distribute each year an amount equal to 8 percent of the value of the trust to one or more charities they selected. The trust was to continue for twenty-four years, after which its assets would continue to be held in trust for Jackie's grandchildren.

Not only would such a trust involve her children in philanthropy, but it also would result in substantial tax savings. The savings arise from the fact that the present value of the 8 percent annuity payable to the charities for twenty-four years would have been an estate tax deduction for purposes of determining Jackie's estate taxes. The exact value of Jackie's estate has not been made public. The *New York Times* reported that her executors had valued her estate at $43.7 million but that the amounts paid at auction for some of her property had led to an IRS audit to determine if the value wasn't closer to $73 million. No matter what the value, actuarial tables published by the IRS disclose that Jackie's estate would only have had to pay estate taxes on about 3 percent of the value of the assets that would have gone to the charitable income trust. However, Jackie's will did not automatically create the charitable income trust. Instead, her will gave John and Caroline the option to inherit her assets directly and pay the estate taxes or allow those assets to pass into the charitable lead trust, save estate taxes, and eventually have those assets pass to their children. According to a December 21, 1996, story in the "Metropolitan" section of the *New York Times*, "The children have apparently determined that it makes more financial sense for them to pay the estate taxes and invest the balance."

Nonetheless, many of our clients view a charitable income trust as the home run of family philanthropic planning. The trust allows them to involve their children in philanthropy by having them serve on an advisory board that picks the charities that receive distributions each year. They are able to involve their children in money management by making them cotrustees or by having them attend periodic meetings with the investment counselors. For parents who are concerned about providing their children with "too much" income while they are young, the trust acts as a form of retirement plan, providing the kids with benefits twenty or thirty years in the future. Just as significantly, the charitable income trust can offer a significant tax saving.

Social Capital

If you are fortunate to have a substantial net worth, you need to think about what should happen with your social capital. Social capital is that part of your estate that your heirs are not going to inherit. Either the government gets it in the form of taxes or you can give it to charities you want to support. If you want to give some or all of your social capital to the government rather than to charity, don't feel bad; you are in very good company. In 1904 one of America's greatest jurists, Supreme Court Justice Oliver Wendell Holmes, described taxes as "the price we pay for a civilized society." Some of our most affluent clients have taken Justice Holmes' comment to heart and have told their families that they consider it morally correct for a portion of their net worth to pass to the government when they die.

For those of you who wish to pick the organizations that will spend your social capital, consider leaving a portion of your estate to a family foundation or a donor-directed fund administered by a community foundation. Both of these provide you with an opportunity to involve your children in selecting charities to which the family will contribute money or time. Consider forming an advisory board and asking interested children or grandchildren to participate (we've seen kids as young as eight years old benefit from this experience).

The Four Most Common Trust Fund Mistakes

Most parents set up trust funds for their children out of noble motives. Their intention is not to put their children on easy street or to curry favor with them. Instead, the goal is usually to pass on family wealth in a responsible way. Despite these noble motives (or perhaps because of them), parents often find themselves making mistakes in how they set up the trusts. Here are the most common ones:

1. **Hiding the trust's existence from children.** Parents mistakenly believe that what their children don't know won't hurt them. They rationalize that they won't create spoiled trust–fund kids if their kids don't know they have a trust fund. The problem, of course, is that they eventually will discover they have one and be confused and upset about why their parents never informed them of it. Or they may learn of its existence inadvertently when they're relatively young and feel deceived and mistrusted.

Early on (even before adolescence), tell your kids about the trust fund and explain that the trust has been established for them as a responsible member of the family. Talk to them about the meaning of the word *trust*. They need to understand that the money they will receive is a sign of your trust in them to use the money wisely and well.

2. **Assigning children recipient–only roles.** In other words, you don't allow your kids to participate in the management of the trust. Perhaps you do this because you're afraid they'll make bad decisions; you don't believe they possess sufficient knowledge to participate in the management process. It's also possible that you don't believe this a relevant role. You're convinced that this is a detail of life they don't need to waste time on. Ultimately, however, they're going to have the authority to invest the trust's money, and when they do, they may use it unwisely.

Your children should learn to manage the trust's money. Explain that one of the responsibilities of having money is learning how to take care of it. Even at a young age, they can become involved as learners. Impress upon them that at some point in the future, it's going to be their money, and they have a responsibility to learn how to invest it and to teach their children in turn. At the very least, if they have no interest in being involved in money management on a day-to-day basis, they need to know enough to be able to interview, evaluate, and monitor competent money managers. This is the type of mature attitude that can be fostered through involving them in trust management.

3. **Creating a trust that is pure legal boilerplate.** Most lawyers are trained to deal with the technical side of estate planning. Their emphasis is on creating documents that carry out your wishes in a tax-efficient manner. If you don't insist upon it, they won't create an estate plan that communicates your values to your children. You should show your family mission statement to your lawyer and explain your wish to have the plan reflect your values. If he says it's impossible to do what you ask, get another opinion. Good estate plans should be flexible enough to accommodate your particular family mission.

4. **Failing to use the trust's capacity to encourage positive behavior.** Properly drafted, trusts can encourage such goals as education, entrepreneurship, and involvement in philanthropy. Nonetheless, parents sometimes think that trusts are not the proper place for specific goals and requirements. They worry that their children will think them mean-spirited or overly controlling. In fact, most children will not resent behavior-related clauses if the clauses reflect values that their parents communicated to them all their lives and if they are fair. Obviously, you don't want to include a clause that prevents your child from receiving any money unless he's a self-made millionaire before age twenty-five or that demands he never touch a drop of liquor. On the other hand, it's perfectly fair to include stipulations about finishing college if education is an important family value or about being employed if a good work ethic is part of your family's belief system. If you include such stipulations, you also have to provide for

what happens if the children don't reach these goals. Do the children get their inheritance at a later age, or does it go to charity? If children are aware of the trust's requirements from the time they're young, they will likely view these requirements as reasonable goals rather than unreasonable limitations.

When Grandparents' Plans Are Not So Grand

If you adopt an estate plan that is based on your family mission statement and designed to provide incentives for responsible behavior, you should share that information with other family members who are likely to make gifts or leave property to your children. Typically, this means your kids' grandparents, as well as childless uncles and aunts. Your plans to raise fiscally responsible kids can be sabotaged by grandparents who create trusts that provide them with big bucks at age eighteen. In our experience grandparents have almost invariably been willing to modify the provisions of their estate plans dealing with their grandchildren when asked to do so by their adult children.

What do you do when the grandparents are unwilling to change a provision that you consider unwise, or when such a trust has already been created for your children by their grandparents or other relatives? Assuming that the trust cannot be modified, you have to face the reality that your child is going to have access to more money at an earlier age than you might wish. Your only choice is to try to apply the old saying that if you are stuck with lemons, try making lemonade. How do you go about making the lemonade? Try to interest your child in money management at an early age. If significant sums are involved, offer to help the child find someone to manage the money for her and establish a reasonable budget. Make certain that your child has some passion in life to follow, whether it is completing his education, joining a band, traveling, or becoming a professional skateboarder. Otherwise, you have a young adult with no interests and no need to go to work to support himself. Our experience has been that boredom plus money may contribute to behaviors that fly in the face of parents' values and lead to unhappiness on the part of the children.

10

Parenting in an Age of Change

Dealing with New or Unusual Money Situations

To say that the typical family no longer fits the "Ozzie and Harriet" model is an understatement. The divorce rate is more than 50 percent. So many divorced men and women remarry that the blended family outnumbers all other kinds of families. Adoptions by single parents and by gay or lesbian couples are becoming increasingly common. Parents of high school kids now have to worry about credit card abuse in addition to substance abuse. College graduates are living at home or in apartments subsidized by their parents because they can't find the "right" job.

These and other developments pose a variety of challenging situations for parents that require Solomon-like decisions. The ones we've found particularly vexing for affluent parents are listed here:

- Lifestyle-changing divorces
- Financial confusion involving stepchildren and adopted children
- Credit card abuse
- Launch of dependent adult children
- Financial relationships with the sufficiently launched adult child
- Newly acquired wealth
- Grandparents as money mentors or monsters

Lifestyle-Changing Divorce

If you are faced with divorce—and statistics give you a fifty-fifty chance—you should try at all costs to avoid turning it into an economic battleground in which the children are among the casualties. Divorce generally has a negative economic impact on families no matter what their financial circumstances might be. It can be especially devastating to children in affluent families, for whom the lifestyle "fall" is often more precipitous than in less-well-off families. Parents can often no longer afford private school or various types of lessons; they may even have to move from a very nice neighborhood to one not as nice. It's also confusing for children when the custodial parent has to struggle and pinch pennies while the other parent seems to maintain an affluent lifestyle. Depending on the age of the children and the developmental stages they're in, divorce can have a significant impact on their money relationships. Your children are still going to be faced with the challenges of passing through each of Erikson's developmental stages, discussed in Chapter 2, but now in the context of having lost an intact family.

If you want to minimize the adverse effect of divorce on your children, both parents have to approach the divorce, in the words of Constance Ahrons, author of *The Good Divorce*, without malice and with a mutual concern for the well-being of the children. If you're divorcing or divorced, consider taking the following steps to prevent the economic fallout of the divorce from harming your child's development:

• Communicate with your child about why and how a less-affluent lifestyle is necessary, and allow her to express her feelings about this fact. If you need to move to a less-attractive neighborhood or otherwise reduce your standard of living, explain to your child what's happening. No question, some kids will be angry at

SILVER NUGGET

Delay reentry into the workforce as long as possible after the divorce if you have young children, because they're "losing" both parents if one spouse moves out and the other goes back to work.

having to give up their private school or the swimming pool at their old house, and they need an opportunity to vent this anger. Allow them to tell how angry they feel, and let them ask questions about why the divorce was necessary. You might also share with them your plan for increasing your income (going back to school to get a degree, getting a job or a better job, etc.) and your ideas for part-time jobs that they might find so that they understand that the current situation may be unpleasant but is not necessarily permanent.

• Be aware of the potential problems in handing off parenting responsibilities to a nanny, au pair, or day-care center. A stay-at-home parent may be forced by economic realities to go back to work after the divorce. Although this may be unavoidable, exercise caution in whom you choose to take care of your child (especially if he or she is very young). Refer back to our discussion of developmental stages and the appropriate use of nannies, au pairs, and day-care centers in Chapter 2.

• Establish a college fund for the children before dividing the property. This will avoid fights over who pays and for what. If it is not feasible, consider the approach taken by Meg and Steve when they divorced. Meg had given up work and stayed home with the children throughout the marriage. Steve was a successful doctor. Meg returned to the workforce after the divorce. Child support ended when the children reached age eighteen. Steve's income then substantially exceeded his ex-wife's. Instead of asking Meg to split the cost of college with him, Steve decided to pay 100 percent of the college expenses of his children. The other side of the coin was Debbie and Richard. Both were professionals and both used their children's college education as a means of getting back at each other. Debbie told the children to ask Richard for college financial assistance because he made more money. Richard told them to ask Debbie for the money because "she couldn't possibly have spent all the child support I paid her."

• Avoid trying to buy your way into favorite parent status. Many divorces result in economic disparity between the former spouses. The parent with the higher income should avoid giving the children things in an effort to prove that he loves them more than the other parent.

Financial Confusion Involving Stepchildren and Adopted Children

Centuries ago, Samuel Johnson observed that "to marry again represents the triumph of hope over experience." If Johnson's observation is true, current statistics suggest that most of us are incurable optimists. About 75 percent of divorced women and 79 percent of divorced men remarry. Sixty percent of the remarriages involve spouses who had children by prior marriages. There are currently more stepfamilies than intact first marriages. Adoptions, too, are increasing. According to the U.S. Department of Health and Human Services, 33 percent of adoptions through the Foster

Care Program are now by single parents. In addition, gays and lesbians are now part of this adoption trend.

Both stepchildren and adopted children pose significant money issues. Typically, the new family experiences anger, jealousy, and resentment if significant alimony or child support or both is being paid. Harry and Sally are great examples. Harry was a dentist, and Sally worked in public relations. They had been married for fifteen years and had a ten-year-old son. For the last five years, they had been fighting over their estate plan. Harry had a nineteen-year-old son and a seventeen-year-old daughter by his first marriage who lived with his ex-wife. Harry had been paying $2,000 a month in child support for his children. When his son reached age eighteen, Harry became responsible for his college education, which was costing about $20,000 a year. Harry and Sally were worth about $3,000,000. Because they lived in a community property state, each owned half. Harry wanted his three children to wind up with his half of the estate after he and Sally passed away. Sally absolutely refused to go along with any plan that resulted in Harry leaving two-thirds of his share of their joint assets to his two older children and only one-third to their child. It didn't matter to her that Harry had three children and she had one. She kept repeating that they had been paying child support for his two kids ever since they had been married, and she wasn't going to agree to give them what she felt was an excessive amount.

Extra people and extra pressures push and pull at the stepfamily. Value systems, decision making, child rearing and discipline are all affected. In the introduction to her book *Funny Sauce*, Delia Ephron provides a perceptive, tongue-in-cheek description of the extended family created by divorce and remarriage:

> We owe the return of the extended family, albeit in a slightly altered form, to an innovation called joint custody, in which two formerly married people share in raising their

children. Your basic extended family today includes your ex-
husband or -wife, your ex's new mate, your new mate, possibly your new mate's ex, and any new mate that your new
mate's ex has acquired. It consists entirely of people who are
not related by blood, many of whom can't stand each other.

Ephron left out an important player and a cause of a great deal
of emotional stress: the stepgrandparent and his or her will.
Grandparents frequently have loyalty conflicts when faced with
stepgrandchildren, especially when they have their own biological grandchildren. And these conflicts are often exhibited in the
grandparent's estate plan, with the grandparents making substantial economic distinctions between biological grandchildren and
stepgrandchildren.

Grandparents who make economic distinctions between biological grandchildren and stepgrandchildren can cause serious
problems. Bruce's parents died in a plane crash twenty years ago.
They left a substantial amount in trust for Bruce and what their
wills called his "natural" children. Bruce and Inez were married
fifteen years ago and have twin sons, Jay and Tony, age twelve.
Inez has a seventeen-year-old daughter, Julie, by her first marriage.
Bruce helped raise Julie since she was a toddler and thinks of her
as his daughter. We were recently consulted by Bruce and Inez.
They were trying to deal with the fact that the twins were going
to benefit from Bruce's trust but Julie would not. How should they
explain this to the children? How could they compensate for this
inequity among the children? What would the effect be on the
relationships among the children?

We recommended that they explain to all three children that
remarriage and adoption were less common when Bruce's parents
were growing up, and their will failed to deal with the possibility
that Bruce would have a stepchild. We also recommended that
Bruce purchase enough insurance on his life to provide Julie with
an equal inheritance.

The "grandparent problem" also occurs with adopted children and stepchildren. Does your parents' will distinguish between adopted grandchildren and biological grandchildren? Does your will make a similar distinction? Estate-planning lawyers don't always raise this question with their clients when they draft wills. Wills often contain a definition of "children" and "grandchildren" buried somewhere in the technical provisions of the document that was never discussed but that can have a lasting negative impact on your family.

Credit Card Abuse

In a very real sense, credit cards are a symbol of the affluent adolescent. Parents give them to their kids with the best of intentions—they tell them it's for emergencies only or give them a monthly limit—but kids sometimes end up abusing the privilege. The nightmare scenarios involve adolescents maxing out their cards, parents rescuing the kids by paying off thousands of dollars of debt, and the situation repeating itself. When this happens, parents communicate to their children that there's no need to be responsible about money management; they also encourage irresponsible behaviors in that the offspring believe that their parents will always rescue them.

We're not against credit cards for kids. Far from it, because these cards can provide very useful learning experiences in money management. But without forethought and discussions with your children, handing them a credit card can be trouble. In addition, this is a relatively new phenomenon because most parents never had these cards when they were teenagers.

Until 1990 credit card companies marketed almost entirely to adults with full-time jobs. College students were considered bad risks; they usually had difficulty obtaining a credit card until they graduated, and even then their parents often had to sign before they could receive cards. Still, this first credit card was the rite of passage between childhood and adulthood for many affluent students. This all began to change in the mid-1980s, as credit card companies decided to extend credit to college students based on their earning potential and removed the requirement of parental cosigners. Today, sixteen-year-old high school students are bombarded with credit card applications, and Barbie dolls come with play credit cards!

The result is not unexpected: increased credit card abuse and personal bankruptcies among the young. According to Robert D. Manning, author of *Credit Card Nation*, average credit card debt for college students more than doubled between 1990 and 1995. The American Bankruptcy Institute reports that personal bankruptcies filed by persons age twenty-five or younger increased almost 500 percent between 1993 and 1998.

By the time your child is a high school junior, she will probably have asked you if she can get a credit card. So what should you do? Co-sign or refuse until your child is older? If your sixteen- or seventeen-year-old has demonstrated that she is reasonably responsible with money, we recommend that you use a credit card as another means of helping your children learn about money. *Reasonably responsible* means that she has demonstrated an ability to spend within the confines of an allowance and is not constantly asking to borrow money or saying things like, "I owe my friend $50 that she lent me to get this sweater I really wanted, and she's mad because I haven't been able to pay her back." Here are three indications of reasonably responsible children: (1) participated in family philanthropic efforts; (2) worked at part-time summer jobs and saved their income for a specific purpose; and (3) generally mirrored family values in relationship to money.

We've found that the following four-step process is a good way to maximize the learning potential inherent in giving your child a card.

1. **Explain the importance of a good credit history.** Without good credit, your child will find it impossible to rent a car, lease an apartment, or purchase anything over the phone or through the Internet. Your child needs to understand that it is far worse to have a bad credit history than no credit history at all. We know some parents who simply co-sign for a credit card in their child's name with a low ($100 to $200) limit, use the card once a month to make a $10–$20 purchase, and pay the statement in full each month. Although this practice will insure an excellent credit rating, it won't help him learn anything.

2. **Do a trial run.** Make sure that your child has a checking account and has learned how to write a check and balance the account. Then get him a debit card, which looks like a credit card but is tied to the checking account. If the checking account does not have overdraft protection, the amount that can be charged on the debit card is limited to the amount in the account. This avoids the possibility of a spending spree when your child is first learning about credit cards. Understand that a spending spree is a real possibility, no matter how responsible your child might seem. Imagine handing your child $5,000 in cash and telling him that he can only spend $100 of it. There is going to come a time when your child will be sorely tempted to exceed this limit. The same thing will happen when you give him a credit card with a $5,000 maximum. Therefore, start out with the debit card and see how he does. As an alternative, get your child a prepaid credit card, such as the Visa Buxx card, which allows the parents to control the card's limit.

3. **Debunk the myth of easy credit.** Once you feel your child is sufficiently responsible to have a credit card, you need to educate your child about the real cost of credit. Read the credit card application and determine the annual percentage rate (APR). Explain to your child how interest accrues and increases the cost of what is being purchased if the entire balance is not paid every month. Whether the card can be paid off every month is a function of your child's income (allowance plus any income from discretionary chores or a part-time job) and the amount charged on the card. If the card will not be paid off every month, set a dollar limit that is appropriate for the card. Make sure your child understands the connection between charging one month and paying the bill the next month. Teach your child about late fees. The credit card issuer may charge $25 for a late payment, even if the balance is only $10! Stress the importance of keeping the card safe, and help your child figure out what to do if the card is lost or stolen.

4. **Monitor your child's use of the credit card.** Review the statement monthly and discuss purchases. This serves two purposes. First, you can observe whether your child is handling the card responsibly. Is she paying the full amount each month? Is she incurring late charges? Is she using the card for inappropriate purchases, such as a $5 charge for fast food that she could have paid out of pocket? Second, it's an opportunity to observe and discuss the pattern of purchases. It's eye-opening for kids to realize that they're spending their entire allowance on gas for the car each month or that they are single-handedly keeping the local clothing store in business. Credit card statements can't be rationalized away or denied; they offer clear evidence of spending patterns. Don't use them to berate your child for poor judgment. Instead, employ the statement as a launching pad for a discussion of whether this is the best way for her to use her purchasing power.

Silver nuggeT

Write down what you would have bought if your parents would have given you a credit card when you were sixteen. Is it different from what your children are buying?

Launching Dependent Adult Children

Launching children into the world has become an increasingly challenging activity for parents, especially parents from middle- or upper-income households. Adult children who are insufficiently launched—that is, who are not prepared to take on adult responsibilities—create significant problems for themselves and their parents, and many of these problems relate directly or indirectly to money issues. Even sufficiently launched young adults, however, encounter some financial issues that parents often must confront.

In the mid-1980s sociologists and psychologists began to recognize a new phenomenon, prevalent primarily among children of affluent parents: many children born after the '60s were taking a decade longer than any previous generation to assume adult responsibility. Susan Littwin, the author of *The Postponed Generation: Why American Youth Are Growing Up Later*, was among the first of the popular commentators to report on this phenomenon. Littwin pointed out that many children of affluent boomer families were overprotected. To many boomers, good parenting meant giving their children the material possessions the boomers often lacked while growing up and protecting them from the stresses of failure and disappointment that are inherent in growing up. These protected children were shielded from the normal childhood problems that are necessary stepping-stones in the process of learning to cope with reality. They attained adulthood in families where, in the words of Littwin, the parents continuously "smoothed out the wrinkles."

In 1989 sociologists Allan Schnaiberg and Sheldon Goldenberg, coauthors of "From Empty Nest to Crowded Nest: The Dynamics of Incompletely Launched Young Adults," coined the term *incompletely launched young adults* to describe this phenomenon. They pointed out that many boomers had not prepared their children to become responsible, self-supporting adults. As a result, they were either staying home in droves or living in apartments subsidized by their parents. Between 1964 and 1989, there had been more than a 25 percent increase in the number of adult children between ages twenty and twenty-four living at home, and more than a 50 percent increase in the number of adult children between ages twenty-five and twenty-nine living at home.

If these young adults moved out, however, they often received help from the parents and resented it. Adults, unlike young kids, resent being dependent, and this is true whether they live at or away from home. Paradoxically, these young adults reacted to this support by rebelling against their parents. When they rebelled—by abusing alcohol or drugs, getting in financial trouble, and so forth—they often needed to be rescued by parents. Littwin refers to this cycle as "rebellion-and-rescue dependency."

As a result of these trends, many insufficiently launched middle-class young adults came to exhibit that narcissistic sense of entitlement that was once the exclusive province of children of the very rich. They identified with their parents' upper-middle-class lifestyles, but not with their upper-middle-class work ethic. They expected to enjoy the comfortable lifestyle of their parents once they were on their own, but they had no comprehension of the concept of "paying their dues" to obtain it.

If you have a college graduate who just cannot find the right job, or a twenty-year-old who has dropped out of college, likes living at home, sleeping late, and partying all night, you are probably tearing your hair out trying to figure out how to get him properly launched into the world. We've spent a few pages describing this phenomenon in part because you should be aware that you're not to blame and that societal trends have contributed greatly to this situation. So stop beating yourself up, and start taking the steps that will free your child both economically and psychologically. Specifically, wean your adult child from family support and limit rescuing.

This can be a slow process, as the following example demonstrates. Christina was second-generation wealth. Her parents had run a successful business on the East Coast before moving to California to retire. They had established trusts for all of their children, and Christina had never needed to work. When she began seeing Eileen (one of the authors) for therapy, Christina expressed concern about her relationship with her adult daughter. Christina was wondering whether she was doing the right thing in supporting her twenty-five-year-old daughter, Jessica, to the tune of $6,000 a month so that she could attend graduate school full time, lease a condominium in Brentwood, and not have to work. "Am I going to turn Jessica into someone with the same self-doubts I have?" she asked. Over several months, Christina came to the conclusion that it was necessary to start reducing and eventually eliminating the support payments. But she was afraid to confront Jessica alone. Fortunately for Christina, she was working with a bright and empathic financial advisor who offered to help. Jessica was invited to meet with the two of them, and the financial advisor explained that Christina was going to phase out support payments over the next five years. Jessica was hysterical. How could they do this to her? How could she support herself? The financial advisor offered to help Jessica develop a budget, a concept she had never seriously entertained previously. They met again the next

year. There were sobs, but the hysteria was absent. At the end of
the five-year phaseout, Jessica was delighted that Christina had
forced her to learn to stand on her own two financial feet. Jessica
had her graduate degree, a full-time job, and was entirely self-supporting. Just as important, Jessica had matured into a responsible
adult who enjoyed a more rewarding relationship with Christina
as well as other people.

Unlike Christina, you may be one of the lucky ones and be able
to wean your child at a much faster pace. Ed and Marcia's daughter, Patty, had always been interested in local politics. In her junior
year, she dropped out of college, moved back home, and
announced that she had accepted an unpaid internship in the
mayor's office. Ed and Marcia reviewed their options and decided
to tell Patty that they were opposed to her decision to drop out of
college but that she could live at home and they would support her
for six months. At the end of six months, she would have to have
a paying job and an apartment. They had expected their daughter
to protest; they had anticipated the sort of temper tantrums that
she had thrown as an adolescent when she felt she was being
"deprived" of things their family wealth "entitled" her to. To
their surprise, however, Patty agreed with their terms and before
the six months were up, she had a full-time job with the city and
had moved to her own apartment. They said, "It's as if she's grown
up before our eyes."

As a parent, you're going to need to demonstrate the strength
of your convictions. Just because your child is an adult doesn't
mean he will refrain from using adolescent manipulation. A common problem is when parents give deadlines and their children
ignore them, assuming that they can push the limits just as they
did when they were younger. In these situations, you have to be
prepared to follow through. Letting adult kids off the hook does
them more harm than good. Greg, age twenty-four, had returned
home after graduating from an Ivy League college to look for a

job as a screenwriter. Greg's parents, Paul and Amanda, owned a large home in Beverly Hills with a guest cottage in back. Greg settled into the guest cottage and began a cursory search for a job. After six months went by without Greg finding a job suitable to his talents (although he developed a fine tan by spending a lot of time in the family swimming pool), his parents started to suggest that he really needed to move out, find a job, and start supporting himself. Greg agreed. His tan improved, but still there was no job that he felt was a "really good fit." Finally, on May 1, Paul and Amanda told Greg that he needed to move out by August 1. "Oh, yeah, no problem," was the reply. They reminded Greg once in June. On August 1 at 8:00 A.M. the movers arrived. Greg couldn't believe it. They packed up his clothes and personal possessions and moved Greg to a motel several miles away. Paul and Amanda reassured Greg that they had prepaid the rent for the next two weeks. By the third day, Greg had a full-time job at a PR firm. Although it was not his dream job, it would pay the bills while he pursued his writing career.

The odds are that if you've followed many of the tenets of this book, you won't have to resort to forcefully launching your child out of the house and into a motel. Some of you, however, will have arrived at this book when your child is already a late adolescent or a young adult and will be dealing with a son or daughter who is resisting financial independence. If so, you may have to bite the bullet and give them a little push. You're going to have to be the judge if they're ready for that push. Some young adults just aren't ready emotionally to make it on their own and need to do more growing up before they can be launched. Others, however, are simply happy to bask in the affluent lifestyle you've made possible. Remember, they've enjoyed the nice house, good meals, big-screen television, great stereo, and all the other amenities for many years. These adult children who have been able to avoid fiscal responsibility may find it a hard habit to break. In addition, some adult children are scared of financial independence even if they don't show it. They may worry about their ability to acquire, use, and manage money. It's not necessarily that they're bad kids or even lazy ones, but they're apprehensive about their ability to make it financially in the outside world. You know your adult children better than anyone, and if they seem as if they're emotionally ready to be on their own—and if their values are good and strong—then you may want to toss them into the water.

SILVER NUGGET

Anticipate how you might avoid rescuing your child if she gets herself in financial trouble; write down what you can do or say to communicate to your child that she's capable of rescuing herself.

But what if it appears that they can't swim? Unless they're really drowning, don't rescue them. Expect them to have some financial problems; many young adults do. They're going to fret about the amount of their credit card debt and the cost of their car payments; they're going to moan about how they've been eating pasta five nights a week and rarely get to go out and have a decent meal. Let them wail and moan; invite them over to the house for a good meal or take them out. If necessary, give them cash for Christmas, Hanukkah, and birthday presents (but not so much that it pays off all their debts or helps them avoid working). Premature rescuing sends the wrong message; it communicates that you don't believe they're capable of being financially independent, and you're the one they believe. Giving your child enough money to live on for a year or paying off their cars and other debts makes them feel like a dependent child. They need to convince themselves that they're capable of functioning on their own, and the best way to do that is to struggle financially for a while and eventually come out on top.

Financial Relationships with the Sufficiently Launched Adult Child

At last your children have moved out and are on their own. You couldn't be prouder of them; they have good values and seem to have healthy money relationships. You have successfully raised a child in an affluent environment and now you don't have anything left to do, right?

Not necessarily. You still have a role to play that can have a positive impact on your child's money relationships.

There is no "correct" approach to dealing with your adult children once they have been launched and are on their own. Some parents provide no support for their adult children. Others pay for education but nothing else. Others make substantial gifts. None of these approaches is inherently right or wrong. It is simply your parental style. And all of the approaches can produce mature, responsible adult children. Giving relatively little to your children is unlikely to hamper them. On the other hand, we know families who have provided financial support for their adult children well into their forties without harming them.

We suggest that you should keep the following points in mind when dealing with your adult children.

• Help your child financially without hurting her. If you're a boomer, recognize that times have changed since you were growing up. In the late '60s, the cost of a nice apartment in L.A. might have been 30 percent of your take-home pay when you were just starting out in an entry-level position. Today that same apartment might equal or exceed your child's take-home pay for the same entry-level position. Your sufficiently launched adult children might need some economic help for a short period after they graduate from college and become employed. One of the pleasures of affluence is being able to help our children in a constructive way. The key is helping them in a way that doesn't make them dependent or communicate that you think they can't make it on their own. For this reason you need to help your child understand that she can't expect to enjoy the same lifestyle on her own that she enjoyed while living at home. A nonjudgmental talk about budgeting and making financial choices as a rite of passage that everyone goes through is worth having. Lending them a relatively small amount of money is fine, as long as they understand that you're not going to make a habit of it or that it's designed for them to spend on a luxury (as opposed to a necessity).

• Articulate your money value system as it applies to adult children; let them know what you are going to pay for and what you won't. From the very beginning of their leave-taking, communicate the parameters of your largesse so you avoid unmet expectations. The last thing you want is for them to leave home believing that you're going to pay for X, Y, and Z when you're only going to pay for X. If your child is going to college or graduate school, clarify whether you'll pay for a dormitory or for an off-campus apartment. If they're done with school, talk about if you'll help them with the down payment on a house or assist them in going into business. Define your terms and conditions so that they're in line with your values. Your approach is going to vary depending on your values and the type of child you have. For some of you it's going to make more sense to give them relatively little because they're the type of kids who need to believe in themselves and their ability to make it on their own. On the other hand, you may have a very mature, responsible child who has chosen a profession that requires an inordinate commitment of time, and she may need more financial assistance to get by during the early part of her profession. You have to be the judge of what is appropriate financial assistance, recognizing that there is no amount that is right or wrong.

• Get "informed consent" from your child. Let your kids know if there are strings attached to any financial aid you might provide and give them the opportunity to say no if the strings aren't acceptable. If you and your spouse give $10,000 tax free to your son and daughter-in-law, is it OK for them to use it for a new BMW or did you intend the money to go into your granddaughter's college saving account?

• Don't use your money to control your kids or to punish them. If this seems obvious while your kids are little, it may not be so obvious when they leave home. Some parents are anxious because they can't control a child who is no longer dependent on them, and they seek (unconsciously) to reestablish that dependence by giving them money. Similarly, some parents are angry at their children for leaving home and withdraw any financial support because they've "deserted" them. Don't make either of these mistakes; think long and hard about why you're giving or not giving your adult children money.

• Let your adult children know that if they request money, it should be for "worthwhile endeavors." For several years we have lectured at the annual New York University Family Wealth Institute. Last year one of the attendees sent us a copy of a letter he had written to his two adult children. It was entitled "Endeavors," and in it he said that he was willing to help them financially by "supporting worthwhile endeavors." He said that in evaluating requests for money, he was looking at several things:

- Is whatever you're going to do important to you? Are you really committed?
- Does it represent something meaningful both to yourself and others?
- Does it move you toward financial self-sufficiency?
- Will money make a difference?
- Is giving you money healthy for our relationship?

He ended the letter with this observation:

> The distinction I guess I would like to draw between giving you money for worthwhile endeavors versus just for the hell of it is the difference between using money I give you to fuel your independence versus using it to prolong your dependency or to take the easy way out.

- Don't forget vocational testing. One of the good news–bad news scenarios for children from affluent backgrounds is that they often have more choices than other kids. Typically, they've had the time and opportunity to explore different interests. Their parents have been able to provide them with various types of lessons that dovetail with their interests and helped them in other ways to develop their talents. It's not unusual for a young adult to be debating whether she should go to law school, join the Peace Corps, or become a white-water-rafting guide. The problem, of course, is that many young adults are bewildered by the many choices available to them. Even the most motivated and responsible young adult occasionally finds himself not sure which occupational or professional track to follow. "There are too many things that interest me. I don't know what to major in." "I'll be graduating in six months and I still don't know for sure what should be my first job." "I've been working at this job for two years and it feels like a dead end. I don't know where to go or what to do." One of your best investments in time (and possibly money) is to suggest that your child undertake vocational testing at a local college or university. According to Stephan Poulter, a clinical psychologist in Los Angeles, the tests you should look for are 16 PF, the Myers-Briggs Type Indicator, and the Strong Interest Inventory.

Newly Acquired Wealth

Imagine that you just came into a large sum of money. Although winning the lottery is an uncommon occurrence, inheriting money is not. It's also possible that a wise investment paid off, an entrepreneurial business venture took off, or you just got a great new job that doubles your salary and includes all sorts of perks. Whatever the cause, you suddenly have boosted your net worth. Naturally, you use this additional money to buy the things you've always wanted. Perhaps you move to a better neighborhood or build your dream house. You might buy a second home or start taking more and better vacations. Some people purchase fancy

SILVER NUGGET

Pretend you just won the lottery. List three major purchases you would make and think about how these purchases might affect your child.

cars, put in swimming pools, join country clubs, and generally increase the quality and amount of what they buy.

As you might imagine, all this changes your lifestyle, and this change can bring stress to both parents and children. If, for instance, you move into an old money neighborhood, you might be viewed with disdain as "nouveau riche." You may send your kids to private schools where they may feel out of place and have trouble adjusting. Some newly wealthy parents feel guilty about being rich and overreact, refusing to spend any money on their children for fear of spoiling them. And there are those parents who do spoil their children, taking advantage of their newfound wealth to buy them every toy they can find, no matter the cost; if kids have been taught that presents have to be earned, not just received, they may feel guilty for receiving gifts they feel they don't really deserve. In short, sudden wealth brings change, and change can be a very stressful event for a family and make parenting a greater challenge.

You may be scoffing at these notions, believing that winning the lottery would not place stress on either you or your children. Consider, however, that psychologists classify stress as either good stress, known as *eustress*, or bad stress, known as *distress*. Getting married, having a child, receiving a promotion at work, or winning the lottery are all examples of eustress; getting divorced, having your business fail, or mourning the death of a loved one are all examples of distress. Unfortunately, our bodies don't make these distinctions. Both good stress and bad stress are treated by our bodies as change, but our ability to cope is what determines how the stress affects us. If you have problems coping with the good stress from winning the lottery or taking on the responsibilities of marriage or children, your body will begin to exhibit sleep disruption, aches and pains, and other symptoms usually associated with bad stress.

From 1995 to 1997 Eileen conducted in-depth interviews with individuals who acquired sudden wealth as the result of Initial

Public Offerings, the lottery or similar gambling winnings, and unexpected inheritances. The amounts involved ranged from $5 million to more than $100 million. She was interested in discovering why some people seem to adapt to sudden wealth with few problems while for others it is a major negative event.

The few published studies of lottery winners and inheritors had found that wealth brought no measurable increase in present or projected future happiness and generally painted a picture of sudden wealth as a negative experience. In one study lottery winners actually scored below accident victims who were partially or wholly paralyzed by their accidents in the pleasure they derived from day-to-day events! A 1995 *New York Times Magazine* article on lottery winners stated that although "there are no statistics on what happens to jackpot winners. . . . [A] growing body of evidence suggests that winning big often brings big, if not ruinous, trouble."

Eileen's study produced a number of findings that are relevant to parents concerned about the impact of sudden wealth on their children.

The good news is that three-quarters of the participants in Eileen's study experienced sudden wealth as a positive event. It's good news because it suggests that there's a way to turn this increased affluence into an event that benefits rather than harms children. Eileen's study, unlike prior studies where sudden wealth had a much more negative effect, focused on participants who were actively involved with their legal and financial advisors. It is quite possible that people who receive appropriate legal and financial counseling have a substantially increased likelihood of experiencing sudden wealth as a positive factor in their lives.

Second, she found that the money messages the participants received from their parents while they were growing up were extremely important. Ninety percent of the participants who experienced sudden wealth as positive had received childhood messages from their parents that it was important to deal with money responsibly and to save some part of whatever they received.

Third, a significant majority of all of the participants viewed their sudden wealth as the cause of negative relationships with siblings. In fact, sibling problems was the reason why some of the participants viewed their sudden wealth as negative.

Fourth, a significant majority of the participants who viewed sudden wealth as positive were introspective. They said such things as: "It [sudden wealth] has given me a lot to think about"; "Wealth is a road to self-awareness. I've been grounding myself, getting comfortable with who I am." The ability to engage in introspective behavior clearly appears to be associated with positive adaptation to sudden wealth.

Fifth, just about all the participants voiced concerns about how their sudden wealth would affect their children. They were worried that having so much money might "ruin" their kids; they also didn't want their wealth to prevent their children from engaging in typical "life struggles"; and some of the parents felt their kids were "embarrassed" by their money and neither the kids nor the parents knew how to talk about it.

Given these findings, we offer people who have come into wealth suddenly the following parenting advice:

• **Evaluate how the sudden increase in wealth is affecting your behavior with your children.** Many people are more anxious, short-tempered, and just plain busy because of this wealth; their kids experience or sense a change in them and feel slighted or somehow responsible for this change. In fact, you may be overwhelmed by the fiscal responsibilities of having this additional money; you're spending countless hours trying to keep track of your new investment portfolio and shopping for various purchases. This can be highly stressful, and you may seem to your children like Midas counting his gold. "All they ever talk about is their money," your kids might be saying behind your back (or they may say it to you directly).

The solution may be to hire financial advisors, who can take much of the burden off your shoulders. Many people aren't prepared for the tax, investment, insurance, and estate-planning issues that come with sudden wealth. Stress can be reduced by turning over some of these chores to experts.

• **Don't allow the source of your increased wealth to be a mystery or a taboo subject for your children.** If your children don't understand why you've suddenly moved to a fabulous new house or why your lifestyle has changed, it's going to bother them. If they're preteens, they may well attribute a number of negative causes to your secrecy—ill-gotten gains, nefarious schemes, and so on. As we've stated earlier, money should not be a forbidden subject. Your children should feel free to satisfy their curiosity and you should feel free to give them honest, clear answers. You want them to be comfortable with money, not suspicious of it. The embarrassment Eileen noted in her study can be lessened if you broach the subject of this sudden wealth with your children rather than waiting for them to come to you. Treat this as another opportunity to exchange feelings, thoughts, and experiences with your children.

• **Maintain your values even if you change your lifestyle.** Sudden wealth is seductive. Even if you change your lifestyle, it's important to continue modeling behaviors that reflect your bedrock values.

• **Think before you act.** Because sudden wealth naturally catalyzes contemplation, reflect on what your sudden wealth means and your options before making major decisions. As we've emphasized earlier, philanthropy is an option to consider, not only because it's a good deed but also because it sends a valuable message to your kids. This and other options begin to make sense once you spend some time reflecting on your windfall and how you can put it to use in a way that dovetails with your values.

Grandparents as Money Mentors or Monsters

We looked at grandparents from a somewhat negative viewpoint earlier when considering the effect of wills and trusts that exclude adopted or stepgrandchildren. Grandparents, however, can also make incredibly valuable contributions to your child-raising efforts.

Grandparents are living longer than ever before, and they have a lot more money. Although U.S. Congressional Budget Office statistics seem to keep changing, in the next two decades the parents of the boomer generation are expected to leave anywhere between $10 trillion and $50 trillion dollars to children, grandchildren, and charities.

Grandparents can either be money mentors or money monsters. We have many friends who have interested their ten- to fourteen-year-old grandchildren in investing by giving them stock as birthday presents. The Stein Roe Young Investors Fund sponsors an annual essay contest for children. The Young Investors Fund specializes in companies familiar to children, such as Disney, Coke, Mattel, and McDonald's. Its quarterly reports feature crayon-style drawings that help young investors understand the multinationals in which it invests. In a recent essay contest, fifth-through seventh-graders were asked to write about the person most influential in helping them learn about money and investing. Five of the nine prizewinners named a grandparent.

Then there are the money monster grandparents. Perhaps the biggest money monster is the grandparent who sabotages his or her children. Newspaper advice columns seem to be perpetually running letters from aggravated parents who wouldn't buy video games, TVs, or toy guns for their children, only to have Grandpa or Grandma show up with the forbidden goods. When grandparents know their adult children's wishes regarding their children and then ignore them, they turn into money monsters.

Here are some simple grandparenting guidelines for you to share with your parents that will help them be money mentors:

- If you give money to your grandchildren, suggest that they spend some, save or invest some, and give some to charity.
- Consider giving them a share or two of stock in their favorite company, perhaps Disney or McDonald's. This can become a continuing project as the grandchildren get older.
- Before giving large-ticket items, or anything possibly controversial, like video games, to your grandchildren, check with their parents and respect their wishes. If the parents feel that the grandchildren should earn the money, consider offering to match part of their earnings or perhaps find real chores around your house that the grandchildren could do to earn the money.

No doubt, the world will continue to change and create a host of new issues for parents to deal with besides the seven discussed here. And as the following chapter will demonstrate, the future is going to make raising a child in an affluent environment that much more of a challenge.

11

Invest in Your Child's Future

It's been said that with power comes responsibility. We'd amend that saying to read, "With the power of money (affluence) comes parenting responsibility." Some of you may feel that there's a great deal to think about and do to raise an emotionally healthy, financially savvy child. Although that's true, it shouldn't be an overwhelming task. One of our goals in writing this book was to facilitate the process. The ideas and tools in these pages should save you both time and grief. Although we've presented many suggestions and concepts, you'll find that even if you only think about and implement some of them, they will make your job as parents that much easier.

It might help, too, if you consider that the book can be summed up in the following four basic recommendations:

1. **Understand the theoretical underpinnings.** Research by John Bowlby and Mary Ainsworth on attachment theory and Erik Erikson's developmental stages provide us with a lens through which we can view the effects that affluence has on us and our children. Recognizing our own relationships with money is also crucial. By being highly conscious of these psychological factors, we can not only avoid sending the wrong money messages to our children, but we can be aware of what the right ones are and when and how to send them.

2. **Live your values.** You may have great bedrock values that aren't communicated—and may even be contradicted—by your money behaviors. By identifying your values and making sure they come through in your money attitudes and actions, you provide a strong defense against the potential negative impact of living in an affluent environment.

3. **Teach your child about money through word and deed.** We cannot overemphasize how important it is to be your child's money mentor. Use allowances, estate planning, credit cards, and other tools to convey valuable lessons about how to use, manage, and acquire money. Rather than turn financial issues into taboo subjects, assure your child that you're always ready, willing, and able to answer money questions.

4. **Raise a giver rather than a getter.** Philanthropy provides wonderful opportunities for us and our children. Truly, by helping others, we help ourselves and our family. Make giving activities central to your family from the time your children are little through young adulthood. Further, make them participatory activities. Active and enthusiastic involvement in good causes goes a long way toward preventing a sense of entitlement and prejudice that is too often found in affluent communities.

These four recommendations are not only relevant now but will apply in the coming years.

Tracking the Money-Related Trends

Although we agree with Casey Stengel's famous comment that it is difficult to make predictions, especially about the future, we're cautiously optimistic. The following trends may have a significant impact—both pro and con—on our ability to raise good, fiscally responsible kids.

The Ever-Expanding Internet

The same technology that has made it possible for the media to urge our children to consume without letup and act on impulse—television—has also made it possible for increasing numbers of concerned individuals and organizations to reach out to our children. The very same can be said of the Internet. In affluent communities everywhere, children and their parents are on-line. More so than in less-affluent communities, families have the money to purchase the type of technology that makes it easier to use the Internet and its resources. No doubt, these resources will grow in number and sophistication in the future, and it's important to keep track of what they are and how they might assist you with specific financial child-raising issues. For now, however, consider a sampling of some sites relating to money and children that we recommend to our clients:

• Organized in December 1995, the Jumpstart Coalition for Personal Financial Literacy is dedicated to teaching young adults the fundamentals of financial literacy. Jumpstart's Reality Check lets your child imagine he is out of the house living on his own and offers a simple check-the-box questionnaire for him to complete. What kind of car is he going to buy? Where will he live? Does he love to go to the movies or to the clubs every weekend? As the website says, "Fill in your choices and then get ready for a reality check! Chances are you'll be surprised by how much your so-called Dream Life is going to cost you." Click on www.jump startcoalition.com/.

• To help your child develop a budget, surf over to The New York Society of CPAs, which offers a form you can use. Click on www.dollar4dollar.com/guides/kidplan.htm.

• The Canadian Imperial Bank of Commerce (CIBC) offers a great website for children and parents. The kids section is divided into under-age-twelve and thirteen-through-eighteen sections. In the under-age-twelve section, children can visit the Money Machine (where they enter how much they intend to save every week and the amount, if any, of their parents' contributions) and the Allowance Room (where they can click on fifteen different toys, ranging from dolls to bicycles, and be told how many weeks it will take them to save up for the item). The age-thirteen-through-eighteen site introduces the children to savings, setting goals, and budgeting. Of course, you shouldn't feel compelled to use the arbitrary age cutoffs employed by CIBC. A mature ten- or eleven-year-old might have a good time in the age-thirteen-through-eighteen site. Click on www.cibc.com/English/personal services/students_and_parents/index.html.

• If you are interested in reading a collection of articles on all aspects of allowances, click on www.kidsmoney.org.

• StudentMarket.com and Consumer Credit Counseling Service of Southern New England have created a website for teenagers and young adults that highlights the importance and implications of handling credit responsibly and establishing a positive credit history. Click on www.studentmarket.com/student market/student-credit-card-basics.html.

• Another website with information on students and credit cards is www.consumeralert.org/pubs/research/Aug99Student Debt.htm.

The Diversity Challenge

An article widely circulated on the Internet and attributed to Phillip M. Harter of the Stanford University School of Medicine puts the world's diversity in perspective:

> If we could shrink the earth's population to a village of precisely one hundred people, with all the existing human

ratios the same, it would look something like the following. There would be:

fifty-seven Asians
twenty-one Europeans
fourteen from the Western Hemisphere, both north
 and south ·
eight Africans
fifty-two would be female, forty-eight would be male
seventy would be nonwhite, thirty would be white
seventy would be non-Christian, thirty would be
 Christian
eighty-nine would be heterosexual, eleven would be
 homosexual
six people would possess 59 percent of the entire world's
 wealth, and all six would be from the United States
eighty would live in substandard housing
seventy would be unable to read
fifty would suffer from malnutrition
one would be near death, one would be near birth
one (yes, only one) would have a college education
one would own a computer

Think of what these statistics mean for our children. Less than 20 percent of the population of the world is literate, with adequate housing and enough to eat. Having a computer in their homes—let alone in their bedrooms—means that our children are among the very elite of the world.

Affluence makes it easy for our children to travel to other countries. Similarly, scholarship programs and grants offered by U.S. educational institutions are making it easier for Third World children to be educated in the United States. As the world truly moves toward becoming a global village, our children are coming into daily contact with people from diverse backgrounds. It won't be long before just about every workforce, school, and other social institution is integrated in the broadest sense of that word. It becomes increasingly important for us to raise our children to value diversity and to understand that affluence simply means that they might have more material goods than others, not that they are better than others. To function effectively in the world, they are going to need to learn how to interact with people without prejudice or misconceptions.

The Quest for Money Heroes in a World of Money Villains

Because the United States doesn't have royalty, the youth of America sometimes turn to the rich and famous as role models. Historically, the rich—usually "old" money that was inherited, rather than earned—made up high society. And Hollywood provided the famous. Together, the rich and famous established fashion, determined which restaurants were in, and provided the occasional scandal for the tabloids. In the last few decades, the entertainment/media/sports complex has created a new class of rich and famous role models for our children: twentysomething athletes and entertainers making millions a year, some of whom are poster boys for drug abuse and criminal behavior ranging from assault and battery to rape and murder. Add to the mix the newest concept of TV "reality" programming, in which lying, cheating, deceiving others, and even being unfaithful are shown as helping the contestants win millions.

We don't see this trend of glorifying immorality slowing down in the years ahead. Short of locking our kids in a closet, never letting them watch TV or listen to the radio, and making certain they have no friends, there is simply no way we can prevent them from being exposed to much of what we view as negative aspects of contemporary culture. Because we can't prevent the exposure, we need to counteract the negative messages they will be receiving by exposing them to role models who exemplify virtues rather than vices, especially when it comes to money.

It is going to become increasingly vital for us to find money heroes and communicate their stories to our children. As we've stressed earlier, many wealthy celebrities, athletes, and business executives are model citizens and use their money to make the world a better place to live in. As your children grow up in the coming years, they need to be aware of their stories and how they chose to use their money in a highly value-conscious manner. By deed rather than word, however, you can be money heroes to your children. Movie producer Sarah Pillsbury, one of the founders of Liberty Hill Foundation, talks about her parents as money heroes, whose examples taught her how to be a good citizen. She, in turn, is being such a role model for her children.

The Desire to Live a Meaningful (and Not Just a Material) Life

Interest in both philanthropy and spirituality is going to increase in the future. As more Americans become affluent, we are beginning to experience what Eileen likes to describe as the "so what syndrome." We're more affluent than our parents; we probably work as many or more hours as they did; we may see our kids less; we enjoy a high standard of living. So what? Are we really happier? Do our lives make more sense? Are our kids happier?

When we begin delving into these questions, we begin to realize that a sense of living meaningful lives is connected to a feeling that we are living lives that involve some measure of helping others, a sense of giving back to society. More and more, we are discovering the need for individual involvement in philanthropy and its beneficial effects on the family and for spending more time with our family, perhaps even at the expense of extra income.

Searching for Time to Parent Properly

For several years, we have been conducting seminars and workshops on the psychology of affluence for families and professional financial advisors. (You can find information about the Gallo Institute and our programs at www.galloinstitute.org.) We have found that parents throughout the United States are increasingly aware of the psychological and emotional aspects of affluence and recognize the need to demystify the role that money plays in their—and their children's—lives. The single greatest tool available for parents to accomplish this goal is time—time spent with their children without an agenda.

Mary Pipher, author of *The Shelter of Each Other: Rebuilding Our Families*, believes that most parents are no longer raising their kids. Instead, the kids are being raised by the media. What the media is teaching our kids is often at odds with our most important values. Most of us attempt to remind our children that there are limits. When they demand a new toy or insist they must have designer clothes, we explain that "there is a word *enough* in the English language," that they are not the center of the universe, that their every need does not have to be gratified immediately, and that it is important for them to learn to delay the need for immediate gratification. But even as we communicate these messages, the media is telling them, in our own homes, "Don't think. Act on impulses."

The key to raising our children—rather than allowing the media to do so—is to be connected with them, sharing what Edward M. Hallowell, a distinguished psychiatrist and author of *Connect*, describes as "the human moment." The human moment is simply two or more people together, paying attention to one another.

But Hallowell and Pipher both point out that we are losing the human moment, especially with our kids, because we're too busy and managing our time too poorly. Today Pipher finds that the problems most families bring into therapy "are directly or indirectly related to time." She spends much of her time treating her patients' schedules and telling her clients that they need to spend time with their kids. The cell phone and beeper are marvelous means for parents to keep in touch with their children, but they are also creating the specter of more communication but less time with our children. Digital communication may be the solution to transmitting vast amounts of business data, but it will never replace face-to-face communication between parent and child in transmitting human values.

At least some of that time needs to be floor time or hanging-out time, where you don't have an agenda and your child "owns" you. During this time, you need to engage in reflective discussion, where you learn how your child thinks and what he thinks. You want to share opinions, attitudes, and ideas that give your child an opportunity to explore your mind while you are exploring his. Together, these combine to create a human moment in which you and your children can relate and live your values, including your money values. It is out of this process that the family soul, a sense of family unity, and a shared value system develops.

Preparing to Parent in the Midst of Plenty

As challenging as it is to be a parent in an affluent environment, the good news is that most parents are up to that challenge. Many of the stories we've told in this book are hopeful ones, stories about people who have used their financial resources to help raise

honest, moral, and financially astute kids. You can do a great deal
to both prevent affluence from being a negative in raising your
child and also to turn it into a positive. In addition, you can use
the techniques in this book to remedy bad situations. As you've
learned, parents can intervene and help kids who are overly materialistic, self-centered, unambitious, and elitist. We've seen and
shared with you remarkable examples of parents who have used
philanthropy, therapy, dinner-table discussions, estate planning,
and other tools to help their troubled kids grow up to be terrific
adults.

Whatever the age of your child or the child-raising situation
you find yourself in, we hope this book will be a highly usable
resource. Whether you're looking for a way to stop your child
from acting like he's better than some of his classmates or some
advice about discussing touchy money issues with him, we trust
that you'll find the information you need in these pages.

With that in mind, we'd like to leave you with this last bit of
advice.

Our lives need to create a narrative in which money is placed
in perspective for our children: money is a tool that helps us enjoy
a full life, provides us with opportunities to give back to the community, and makes it possible to create and treasure day-to-day
human moments with our families.

Appendix

In the interest of making *Silver Spoon Kids* as reader friendly as possible, we've placed some of the more technical information from Chapters 2, 8, and 9 in this Appendix.

For those interested in learning more about attachment, the appendix to Chapter 2 describes Mary Ainsworth's "strange experiment," which is used to categorize the various forms of insecure attachment.

For the Internet savvy, the appendix to Chapter 8 provides our favorite philanthropic websites.

The appendix to Chapter 9 provides examples of various types of "incentive trusts."

Chapter 2: Attachment

To better understand the concept of *secure attachment*, it helps to look at the work of the psychologist who created the term. Mary Ainsworth developed "the strange experiment" as a means of measuring the quality of attachment between a mother (or some other caregiver) and a child. The experiment involved mothers and one- to two-year-old children (one mother and one child at a time) who were placed in a room well stocked with toys. The mother would leave the room for a few minutes and then return. The child's reaction to both her leaving and her return was recorded. Then a friendly stranger would come into the room with the mother and child, and the mother would again leave. The child's reactions to being alone with the stranger were also recorded.

Approximately two-thirds of all the children tested exhibited what Ainsworth called secure attachment. For these children, their mother's presence in the room was all they needed; they used her presence as an anchor, drifting to another part of the room to play happily with a toy. When their mother left the room, they would cry initially but after a few minutes they would stop crying and return to playing. When their mother returned, they would run to her, stay with her briefly, and then wander back to the toys. These children also demonstrated a clear preference for the mother over the friendly stranger.

The other one-third of the children demonstrated what Ainsworth called *insecure attachment*. Insecure attachment manifested itself in two ways. One group of children exhibited insecure-avoidant behaviors: they didn't cry when their mothers left the room and they avoided their mothers when they returned; they also tended to ignore the friendly stranger. These children had learned to overregulate their emotions and their behaviors. The other group exhibited insecure-ambivalent behaviors: They cried when their mothers left the room and continued to cry when she returned. Their attachment with the mother was not sufficiently secure that her return was able to soothe them. These children underregulated their emotions and behaviors.

Another negative repercussion of insecure attachment helps explain why some children become selfish and highly egotistical. Children with insecure attachments experience great difficulty with empathy. They have trouble perceiving how others might feel and think, concentrating instead on their own feelings and what's happening in their immediate presence. One of the concerns we hear from affluent parents is that their kids "don't consider anyone's feelings but their own." Classic spoiled-brat behaviors—acting superior to others, an unwillingness to consider how one's actions might impact others, and so on—can stem from the extremely egocentric mindset resulting from insecure attachment as a young child.

To understand how this is so, consider the experiment performed by Peter Fonagy, a British research psychologist, involving three-year-old children. An adult would hide a piece of chocolate in a box, telling the child that he has to leave now but would come back later to eat it. After the adult left the room, Fonagy would move the chocolate to a basket and ask the child where he thought the adult would look for the chocolate when he came back. Children who had not developed a secure attachment tended to say the basket because their prediction would be based on what was in their minds, not on what others would think. A child with an insecure attachment tends to be egocentric. He has trouble becoming empathic and relating to how others might feel or think. Instead he concentrates on his own feelings and what is happening in his immediate presence. He has difficulty understanding that others have minds of their own and have perceptions that are different from his.

Chapter 8: *Philanthropy*

The Internet is a wonderful source of information about charities of all types. Here are some of our favorite websites:

If you want to get the family involved with Habitat for Humanity, check out their website at habitat.org. They are probably looking for volunteers in your area.

For more information about mentor programs, take a look at the U.S. Department of Education publication "Yes, You Can," which is designed to assist organizations and schools across the country in developing their own mentor program. The Fulfillment Fund is cited as a model program. You can access the publication at www.ed.gov/pubs/YesYouCan.

If you are interested in family foundations, check out the Council on Foundations, www.cof.org.

To get a better understanding of what other family foundations are doing, surf over to the Foundation Center (www.fdcenter

.org/), click on "Grantmaker Info," and then click on "Private Foundations." There, you can access an alphabetical list of family foundations with websites that you can sort either geographically (to see who is doing what in your area) or by subject matter (to see what is being done by family foundations in specific subject areas, such as homelessness or the environment).

The Chronicle of Philanthropy, a newspaper of the nonprofit world: www.philanthropy.com

Philanthropy News Digest, another digest of news of interest to nonprofits and donors: www.fdncenter.org/pnd/current

Philanthropy News Network Online, a look at what's happening in the nonprofit world: www.pnnonline.org/

American Red Cross: www.redcross.org

Salvation Army: www.salvationarmy.org

The Funding Exchange: www.fex.org

The Philanthropic Initiative: www.tpi.org

Create-a-Smile: www.create-a-smile.org

More than Money, a membership-supported nonprofit group founded in 1991 to support people with wealth who want to contribute their money and talents toward creating a more joyful, just, and sustainable world, publishes a wonderful quarterly by the same name. You can find More than Money at www.morethanmoney .org. The winter 1998 issue of *More than Money* contains a wonderful story about the One Percent Club, established by Tom Lowe, a Minnesota businessman. Based on a statistical analysis of published IRS data concerning the income tax returns of Minnesota's 28,000 wealthiest individuals, Lowe discovered that if they gave away 1 percent of their net worth a year, they could increase charitable giving in the state by five times the annual budget of the Minneapolis United Way! Assuming you can make a 7 percent after-tax return on your income-producing assets, giving away 1 percent of your net worth every year means that your net worth will double every eleven years, rather than every ten years. In other words, you can choose to give 1 percent of your net worth every year, without sacrifice, and make a major impact on society.

Chapter 9: Estate Planning

Here is an example of a trust provision that one of our clients used when creating a trust fund for her daughter. She wanted the trust to reflect her money values.

My Daughter's Rights to Income and Principal After She Attains Age Eighteen

After my daughter attains age eighteen, I want this trust to assist her in becoming a responsible and self-supporting member of society. Accordingly, I wish the trustee to administer my daughter's trust as follows:

1. **Distributions for Educational Purposes.** If my daughter is a full-time student at an accredited college, university, vocational school, or similar institution and maintains a grade point average equivalent to C or better, the trustee shall pay for her reasonable educational costs. As used in this paragraph, the term *educational costs* includes tuition, books, fees, supplies, transportation (including the cost of an automobile, maintenance, and repairs; and air fare in connection with travel to and from school or with respect to school functions), and reasonable living expenses. The trustee shall have the absolute discretion to determine the reasonableness and duration of all educational costs. [Note: some of our clients like to place a maximum duration on the number of years of education, such as no more than six years of undergraduate education—which allows their child to change his or her major at least twice—or no more than five years of postgraduate education.]

2. **Income-Matching Distributions.** If my daughter either works full time or is a full-time student at an accredited college, university, vocational school, or similar institution and works part time, the trustee shall pay to her each month an amount equal to her gross income that month. The trustee may require my daughter to provide such tax and/or employment verification, including tax returns, as the trustee deems reasonable to determine her gross income.

3. **Discretionary Distributions.** In addition to distributions for educational purposes or income matching, the trustee may also, in the trustee's absolute discretion, pay to my daughter such sums, if any, as the trustee determines to be reasonable and appropriate, taking into account my strong desire that my daughter, unless disabled, be a responsible and self-supporting member of society. Distributions under this paragraph may be made for any or all of the following reasons:

A. Disability
If my daughter is so disabled, either mentally or physically or both, that she is unable to provide for her support, the trustee shall provide adequate funds for her support, maintenance, education, and health care.

B. Low Income
If my daughter is pursuing a career that is socially responsible but that does not produce a substantial monetary reward, such as a teacher or artist, then in addition to income-matching distributions, the trustee may distribute additional funds to her for her support, maintenance, education, and health care.

C. Care for Others
If my daughter is caring full time for one or more family members, including minor children or other relatives or both, the trustee may distribute additional funds to her for her support, maintenance, education, and health care.

D. Entering Into Trade or Business

If my daughter proposes to enter into, purchase, or engage in a trade or business and the trustee determines, in the trustee's absolute discretion, that she possesses the requisite education and skill and that there is a reasonable likelihood of success, the trustee may distribute to her such funds as the trustee deems reasonable to assist her in such endeavor.

E. Other Situations

Any other situation that, in the trustee's absolute discretion, warrants payments to my daughter, provided that the trustee determines that such payments are in accord with my overall philosophy.

The following is an example of a trust provision used by another of our clients who created a trust for a child and wished to give the trustee a great deal of discretion in assisting the child with "socially responsible" endeavors.

Distributions to Michael Between Ages Eighteen and Thirty-Five

Once Michael attains age eighteen and until he attains age thirty-five, we desire that he not depend upon this trust for his support and maintenance. Rather, we desire that the trustee distribute to Michael such sums from his trust as will assist him in living a socially responsible life. For the guidance of both Michael and the trustee, we are setting forth examples below of activities that we consider socially responsible. Being aware of the constantly changing nature of the world in which we live, we are intentionally not defining such terms as *full time*, *part time*, and *socially responsible* but are instead leaving such determination to the sound discretion of our trustee.

The following examples are not all-inclusive, and there may be other activities in which Michael engages that the trustee may deem to be socially responsible.

A. Attending an accredited college, university, vocational school, or similar institution on a full-time basis for the purpose of obtaining an undergraduate or graduate degree

B. Attending an accredited college, university, vocational school, or similar institution on a part-time basis for the purpose of obtaining an undergraduate or graduate degree while working part time

C. Attending an accredited college, university, vocational school, or similar institution on a part-time basis for the purpose of obtaining an undergraduate or graduate degree while also donating a reasonable amount of time to charitable or philanthropic endeavors

D. Working full time, whether employed by others, self-employed, or as an independent contractor

E. Pursuing a career full time, such as a writer, artist, musician, or performer

F. Either working part time or pursuing a career part time while being involved in charitable or philanthropic endeavors without compensation

G. Pursuing any educational, scientific, or charitable goal on a full-time basis that our trustee determines will make Michael a responsible member of society

H. Caring full time for other family members if such obligation reasonably precludes Michael from earning a living or attending school

Bibliography

Ahrons, Constance R. *The Good Divorce: Keeping Your Family Together When Your Marriage Comes Apart.* New York: Harper-Collins, 1994.

Ainsworth, Mary, and Silvia Bell. "Attachment, Exploration, and Separation: Illustrated by the Behavior of One-Year-Olds in a Strange Situation," *Child Development*, vol. 41 (1970).

Barbanel, Linda. *Piggy Bank to Credit Card.* New York: Crown Trade Paperbacks, 1994.

Barber, Judy G. *Family Money: A Commentary on the Unspoken Issues Related to Wealth.* San Francisco: JGB Associates, 2000.

Blouin, B., K. Gibson, and M. Kiersted. *The Legacy of Inherited Wealth: Interviews with Heirs.* Self-published: 1995. Distributed in the United States by The Inheritance Project.

Bodnar, Janet. *Kiplinger's Dollars and Sense for Kids: What They Need to Know about Money—and How to Tell Them.* Washington: Kiplinger Books, 1999.

Bowlby, John. *A Secure Base: Parent-Child Attachment and Healthy Human Development.* New York: Basic Books, 1988.

Brazelton, T. Berry. *Touchpoints: The Essential Reference.* Cambridge, MA: Perseus Books, 1984.

Brazelton, T. Berry, and Stanley Greenspan. *The Irreducible Needs of Children: What Every Child Must Have to Grow, Learn, and Flourish.* Cambridge, MA: Perseus Books, 2000.

Briggs, Dorothy C. *Your Child's Self-Esteem.* New York: Doubleday, 1975.

Brooks, David. *Bobos in Paradise: The New Upper Class and How They Got There.* New York: Simon & Schuster, 2000.

Collins, Chuck, and Pam Rogers. *Robin Hood Was Right: A Guide to Giving Your Money for Social Change.* New York: W.W. Norton & Co., 2000.

Cortes, Carlos E. *The Children Are Watching: How the Media Teach About Diversity.* New York: Teachers College Press, 2000.

Covey, Stephen R. *The Seven Habits of Highly Effective Families.* New York: St. Martin's Griffin, 1997.

D'Souza, Dinesh. *The Virtue of Prosperity: Finding Values in an Age of Techno-Affluence.* New York: The Free Press, 2000.

Dinkmeyer, Don Sr., Gary D. McKay, and Don Dinkmeyer Jr. *The Parent's Handbook: Parenting Young Children; Parenting Teenagers.* Circle Pines, MN: American Guidance Service, 1997.

Elkind, David. *The Hurried Child.* Reading: Addison-Wesley, 1981.

———. *Parenting Your Teenager.* New York: Ballantine Books, 1993.

Ephron, Delia. *Funny Sauce*. New York: Viking, 1982.

Erikson, Erik. *Identity and the Life Cycle*. New York: W.W. Norton & Co., 1980.

Esposito, Virginia M. *Conscience and Community: The Legacy of Paul Ylvisaker*. New York: Peter Lang Publishing, 1999.

Estess, P., and I. Barocas. *Kids, Money & Values*. Cincinnati: Betterway Books, 1994.

Farber, Adele, and Elaine Mazlish. *Siblings Without Rivalry*. New York: Avon Books, 1987.

Fonagy, Peter. "Psychoanalytic Theory from the Viewpoint of Attachment Theory and Research," *Handbook of Attachment*. J. Cassidy and P. Shaver, eds. New York: Guilford, 1999.

Frankl, Viktor, and Gordon W. Allpert. *Man's Search for Meaning*. New York: Washington Square Press, 1998.

Gilbert, Roberta M. *Connecting with Our Children: Guiding Principles for Parents in a Troubled World*. New York: John Wiley & Sons, 1999.

Glenn, H. Stephen, and Jane Nelsen. *Raising Self-Reliant Children in a Self-Indulgent World*. Roseville, CA: Prima Publishing, 2000.

Gottman, John. *Raising an Emotionally Intelligent Child*. New York: Simon & Schuster, 1997.

Greenspan, Stanley. *Building Healthy Minds*. Cambridge, MA: Perseus Books, 1999.

———. *The Challenging Child*. Cambridge, MA: Perseus Books, 1995.

Hallowell, Edward M. *Connect*. New York: Pantheon Books, 1999.

Holtz-Eakin, Douglas, David Joulfaian, and Harvey S. Rosen. "The Carnegie Conjecture: Some Empirical Evidence," *The Quarterly Journal of Economics*, May 1993.

———. "Sticking It Out: Entrepreneurial Survival and Liquidity Constraints," *Journal of Political Economy*, vol. 102, no. 1, 1994.

Huston, Aletha C., and John C. Wright. "Television and Socialization of Young Children," *Tuning in to Young Viewers: Social Science Perspectives on Television*. T. Macbeth, ed. Thousand Oaks, CA: Sage Publications, 1996.

Imber-Black, Evan, and Janine Roberts. *Rituals for Our Times*. London: Jason Aronson, 1998.

Karen, Robert. *Becoming Attached*. New York: Oxford University Press, 1988.

Levy, John. *Coping with Inherited Wealth*. Distributed in the United States by John Levy. Mill Valley, CA: 1987.

Littwin, Susan. *The Postponed Generation*. New York: William Morrow & Co., 1986.

Manning, Robert D. *Credit Card Nation: The Consequences of America's Addiction to Credit.* New York: Basic Books, 2000.

Matthews, Arlene Modica. *Your Money, Your Self: Understanding and Improving Your Relationship to Cash and Credit.* New York: Simon & Schuster, 1991.

McMillon, Bill. *Volunteer Vacations: Short-Term Adventures That Will Benefit You and Others,* Seventh Edition. Chicago: Chicago Review Press, 1999.

Merrell, Susan Scarf. *The Accidental Bond.* New York: Ballantine Books, 1995.

Millon, Theodore. *Disorders of Personality: DSM-IV and Beyond,* Second Edition. New York: John Wiley & Sons, 1996.

Needleman, Jacob. *Money and the Meaning of Life.* New York: Doubleday, 1991.

Newman, Susan. *Little Things Long Remembered: Making Your Children Feel Special Every Day.* New York: Crown Publishers, 1993.

Parkes, Colin Murray, Joan Stevenson-Hinde, and Peter Marris. *Attachment Across the Life Cycle.* New York: Routledge, 1991.

Pearl, Jayne A. *Kids and Money.* Princeton: Bloomberg Press, 1999.

Pipher, Mary. *The Shelter of Each Other: Rebuilding Our Families.* New York: Ballantine Books, 1996.

Raths, Louis, Merrill Harmin, and Sidney Simon. *Values and Teaching: Working with Values in the Classroom*. Columbus: Merill, 1966.

Reiss, Steven. *Who Am I? The 16 Basic Desires That Motivate Our Action and Define Our Personalities*. New York: J P Tarcher, 2000.

Rist, Ray. "Student Social Class and Teacher Expectations: The Self-Fulfilling Prophecy in Ghetto Education," *Harvard Educational Review*, vol. 40, no. 3, 1970.

Rokeach, Milton. *The Nature of Human Values*. New York: The Free Press, 1973.

Rosenfeld, Alvin, and Nicole Wise. *Hyper-Parenting: Are You Hurting Your Child by Trying Too Hard?* New York: St. Martin's Press, 2000.

Schnaiberg, Allan, and Sheldon Goldenberg. "From Empty Nest to Crowded Nest: The Dynamics of Incompletely Launched Young Adults," *Social Problems*, vol. 36, 1989.

Schniedewind, Nancy, and Ellen Davidson. *Open Minds to Equality*. Boston: Allyn and Bacon, 1998.

Shore, Bill. *The Cathedral Within: Transforming Your Life by Giving Something Back*. New York: Random House, 1999.

Siegel, Daniel J. *The Developing Mind: Toward a Neurobiology of Interpersonal Experience*. New York: The Guilford Press, 1999.

Smith, Hyrum W., and Ken Blanchard. *What Matters Most: The Power of Living Your Values.* New York: Simon & Schuster, 2000.

Stern, Daniel. *Diary of a Baby.* New York: Basic Books, 1990.

Trujillo, Michelle L. *Why Can't We Talk?: What Teens Would Share if Parents Would Listen.* Deerfield Beach, FL: Health Communications, 2000.

U.S. Trust Survey of Affluent Americans. New York: Financial Market Research, 1999.

Index

Abacus Wealth Management, 174
Acquistion of money. *See* Money acquisition
Action plans, 57–58
ADL Resources for Classroom and Community, 147
Administrative trustees, 194, 195
Adopted children, 203, 206–9
Adult children
  discussing estate plan with, 190–91
  launching dependent, 213–19
  relationships with sufficiently launched, 219–23
Advertising, 6, 7, 103, 104
Affluence, 1–15. *See also* Money
  attachment and, 20–22
  defined, 4
  parenting generation gap and, 9–12
  positive and negative effects, 3
  riches vs., 2–6
  troubling trends, 6–9
  virtual, 3
After-school enrichment programs, 165–66
Ahrons, Constance, 204
Ainsworth, Mary, 231, 241–42
Alda, Alan, 168–69
Allowance Room, 234
Allowances, xviii, 104–5, 107, 117–32

appropriate amount, 120–21, 123–25
avoiding reward and punishment with, 129–32
clothing, 124
generation gap in, 10–11
Internet sites, 234
items covered by, 123–25
renegotiating, 125–27
responsibilities associated with, 121–23
rules about spending, 127–29
two basic rules, 118–21
Alternatives Grid, 75–76
American Bankruptcy Institute, 210
American Heritage, 42
American Red Cross, 163, 168, 244
Annuities, 196, 197
Anti-Defamation League (ADL), 147
Artists for a New South Africa, 155
Attachment, 17–22, 231. *See also* Insecure attachment; Secure attachment
  impact of affluence on, 20–22
  promoting, 33
  self-regulation and, 19
  studies on, 241–43
Attachment Across the Life Cycle (Parkes, Stevenson-Hinde & Marris), 22
Attachment figures, 17, 18, 20–22
  defined, 18

important qualities for, 21–22
in trust stage of development, 24,
   33–34
Autonomy (developmental stage),
   25–26, 34
Avoidant style of money
   acquisition. *See* Overregulators,
   in money acquisition

Baby boomers, 2, 9, 213–14,
   219–20, 228
Bankruptcy, 210
Barber, Judy, 186
Beatty, Warren, 181
Becoming Attached (Karen), 22
Bill and Melinda Gates Foundation,
   168
Blanchard, Ken, 67
Bobos in Paradise (Brooks), 67
Bodnar, Janet, 123, 124
Bowlby, John, 18, 231
Brazelton, T. Berry, 96, 97
Bribery, 91
British Trust for Conservation
   Volunteers, 151
Brooks, David, 67
BuBBles Company, 29
Budgeting, 105, 107–8, 124
Buffett, Warren E., 185
Building Healthy Minds (Greenspan),
   96, 97, 103
Bush, George W., 178

California Community Foundation
   (CCF), 170–71
Canadian Imperial Bank of
   Commerce (CIBC), 233–34
Cap'n Crunch episode, 64–65
Carnegie, Andrew, 185
Chaotic money management. *See*
   Underregulators, in money
   management

Charitable income trusts, 196–97
Charity, 153. *See also* Philanthropy
Checking accounts, 106–7
Child support, 206, 207
Children Are Watching, The (Cortes),
   142
Choate, Mary, 98
Chores, 122, 124–25, 130
Chronicle of Philanthropy, The, 244
Classism, 142–43, 144–45
"Classroom of Difference"
   program, 147
Cleveland Foundation, 170
Coadministrative trustees, 194, 195
Collaborative communication, 21
College, paying for, 205–6, 207
Collins, Chuck, 155
Community foundations, 162, 163,
   170–71, 198
Compassion, 27
Competitive individualism, 142,
   143–45
Compulsive overspenders. *See*
   Underregulators, in money use
Computers, 7, 8–9. *See also* Internet
Conduit (nonoperating) family
   foundations, 168
Connect (Hallowell), 238
*Conscience and Community: The
   Legacy of Paul Ylvisaker*
   (Esposito), 169
Consistency, 21
Consumer Credit Counseling
   Service of Southern New
   England, 234
Contradictory behaviors, 28, 112–16
Cookie game, 136–39, 146, 160
Corneille, Pierre, 158
Cortes, Carlos E., 142
Council technique, 174
Council on Foundations, 168, 169,
   243

Create-a-Smile, 175, 244
*Creating the Full-Service Homework
    Center in Your Library*
    (Mediavilla), 166
Credit Card Nation (Manning), 210
Credit cards, xvii, 3, 107, 203,
    209–12, 213
    Internet sites on, 234
    minimizing problems with,
        211–12
Credit history, 211
Custodial accounts, 177–78

Davidson, Ellen, 143, 147
Debit cards, 211
Deep Dish TV, 167
Desires, sixteen basic, 63
Developing Mind, The (Siegel), 98
Developmental stages, 17–36, 85,
    204, 205, 231
    allowances and, 122, 132
    attachment in. *See* Attachment
    description of, 22–32
    philanthropy and, 155
    taking the right steps in, 32–36
Dialogue. *See* Reflective dialogue;
    Talking about money
Distress, 224
Distributive trustees, 194, 195
Diversity, 133–52
    challenge of, 234–36
    eight ways to teach, 145–52
    lack of awareness about, 140–41
    modeling, 147–48
    recognizing income gaps,
        134–40
    school and societal curriculum
        on, 142–45
    training in, 147
Divorce, 203, 204–6
Donor Advised Funds, 171, 198
Dot-com companies, 2–3

Doubt (developmental stage),
    25–26, 34
Douglass, Frederick, 167
D'Souza, Dinesh, 144
Dual-income households, 2

Earnings
    of children, 29–30, 124–25, 210
    connection between costs and,
        146
Ego identity, 31
Electronic media, 8–9. *See also*
    Computers; Television
Elkind, David, 8
Emotional communication, 21–22
Entitlement, sense of, 104, 214
Entrepreneurs, 186
Ephron, Delia, 207–8
Erikson, Erik, 23, 132, 204, 231
Esposito, Virginia M., 169
Estate planning, 177–202
    basics of, 178–81
    grandparents and, 201–2
    incentive-based, 191–93
    philanthropy and, 193, 195–98
    talking to children about, 184–91
    trusts in. *See* Trusts
    values communicated through,
        181–83, 200–201, 245–48
"Estate Planning for the Postponed
    Generation" (Gallo), xv
Estate taxes, 179–80, 196–97, 198
Eustress, 224
Excess, 115

Family Foundation Conference, 168
Family Foundation Library, 169–70
Family foundations, 162, 198
    conduit (nonoperating), 168
    overview, 168–70
    resources, 243–44
Family giving pools, 173–74

Family mission statements, 68,
    69
  in estate planning, 181–82, 183,
    184, 192, 194, 201
  example of, 73–74
Family money values continuum,
    81–82
Feeling felt, 98
Floor time, 96, 97–98, 100, 239
Fonagy, Peter, 243
Ford Foundation, 169
Forger, Alexander, 196
Foster Care Program, 206–7
Foundation Center, 243–44
*Founder's Guide to the Family
    Foundation, A,* 169
Frankl, Viktor, 62
Freud, Sigmund, 187
From Empty Nest to Crowded Nest
    (Schnaiberg & Goldenberg),
    214
Fulfillment Fund, 165, 243
Fund for Southern Communities,
    167–68
Funding Exchange, 150, 166, 167,
    244
Funny Sauce (Ephron), 207–8

Gallo Institute, xvi–xvii, 238
Gates, Bill, 185
Gay and lesbian couples, adoption
    by, 203, 207
Gender-based money management,
    113–14
Generalizations, 148–49
Genograms. *See* Money genograms
Gift taxes, 179–80
Global Citizens Network, 151
Goff, Frederick, 170
Goldenberg, Sheldon, 214
Good Divorce, The (Ahrons), 204
Goodwill Industries, 98

Grandparents, 201–2, 208–9,
    228–29
GRAT (Grantor Retained Annuity
    Trust), 192
Great Depression, 9
Green, Hetty, 4, 42
Greenspan, Stanley, 96, 97, 103
GRUT (Grantor Retained
    Unitrust), 192
Guilt (developmental stage), 26–29,
    34

Habitat for Humanity, 164–65, 243
Hallowell, Edward M., 9, 238–39
Hanging-out time, 97, 239
Harmin, Merrill, 69
Harter, Phillip M., 234–35
Harvard Educational Review, 143
Harvard Medical School, 9
Harvard University, 38
Heaven Can Wait (film), 181
Helms, Edgar, 98
High-tech companies, 2–3
Holmes, Oliver Wendell, 198
Holtz-Eakin, Douglas, 186
Homework centers, 166
Huber, Peter, 144
Human moment, 238–39
Hurried Child, The (Elkind), 8
Huston, Aletha C., 148

Identity (developmental stage),
    31–32, 35, 155
Identity diffusion, 31
Impermanence, 6–7
Incentive-based estate plans, 191–93
Incompletely launched young adults,
    214
Industry (developmental stage),
    29–31, 35, 122, 132
Inferiority (developmental stage),
    29–31, 35, 132

Informed consent, 221
Inheritance, 2. *See also* Estate
    planning
Initiative (developmental stage),
    26–29, 34, 122
Insatiable style of money
    acquisition. *See*
    Underregulators, in money
    acquisition
Insecure attachment, 19–20, 242–43
Insecure relationship with money,
    40–41, 44, 45, 50
Internal Revenue Services (IRS),
    163, 197. *See also* Taxes
International Wildlife Education
    and Conservation, 175
Internet, 99, 233–34, 243–44
Introspection, 226
Irreducible Needs of Children, The
    (Greenspan & Brazelton), 96,
    97

*Jerome Levy Economics Institute
    Report,* 139
Johnson, Lyndon B., 169
Johnson, Samuel, 206
Joulfaian, David, 186
Journal of Political Economy, 186
Jumpstart Coalition for Personal
    Financial Literacy, 233

Karen, Robert, 22
Karoff, Peter, 153
Kennedy, Caroline, 197
Kennedy, John F., Jr., 197
Kessel, Brent W., 174
Kingston Technology, 99
Kiplinger's Dollars and Sense for Kids
    (Bodnar), 123

L.A.'s BEST, 165–66
Lemon game, 146–47

Levy, John, 184, 189
Liberty Hill Foundation, 167, 237
Library work, 166
Lifetime gifts, 179–80, 181, 182,
    184, 188. *See also* Trusts
Littwin, Susan, xv, 213, 214
Lottery winners, 223, 224, 225
Lowe, Tom, 244

McMillon, Bill, 150–51
Malta Youth Hostels Association
    Work Camps, 151
Management of money. *See* Money
    management
Manning, Robert D., 210
Man's Search for Meaning (Frankl),
    62
Marris, Peter, 22
Materialism, 6
Matthews, Arlene Modica, 86
Meaningful existence, 237–38
Mediavilla, Cindy, 166
Menninger, Karl, 150
Mentoring programs, 165, 243
Millon, Theodore, 38
Minimum wage, 140
Minneapolis United Way, 244
Minow, Newton, 8
Misers. *See* Overregulators, in
    money use
Mistakes with money, 101, 105
Mistrust (developmental stage),
    23–25, 33–34
Money. *See also* Affluence
    associating happiness with, 94
    developing a philosophy about,
        73–74
    excessive secrecy about, 93
    list of what children should learn
        about, 71
    list of what is important about,
        70

as the root of all evil, 91
as a taboo subject, 11, 12, 92, 227
time as, 92
Money acquisition, 39, 46, 85, 114
    determining importance of, 44
    family money values continuum
        and, 81
    in genogram, 50
    styles of, 41–42
    values in, 66
Money Diary, 78–81
Money genograms, 49–53
Money heroes, 98–99, 236–37
Money Machine, 234
Money management, 39, 41, 46, 85,
    114
    determining importance of, 44
    family money values continuum
        and, 81
    gender-based, 113–14
    in genogram, 50, 52–53
    styles of, 43
    trusts and, 193–95
    values in, 66
Money messages, 39, 45, 48, 231
    contradictory, 114
    newly acquired wealth and,
        225–26
    teachable times for. *See* Teachable
        times
Money morality, 12
Money narrative, 13–15
Money personalities, 37–58. *See also*
    Money relationships
    balanced, 58
    elements of, 38–43
Money Pie of Life, 77–78, 79, 146
Money-related trends
    tracking, 232–39
    troubling, 6–9

Money relationships, xviii, 85
    changing, 53–58
    comparison of charts, 48
    comparison of past and present
        experiences, 46
    considering money messages, 48
    exercise for, 46–47
    genogram for, 49–53
    rating of, 47–48
    secure vs. insecure, 40–41, 44, 45,
        50
    working on, 43–50
Money use, 39, 41, 46, 85, 114
    determining importance of, 44
    family money values continuum
        and, 81
    in genogram, 50, 51, 52
    styles of, 42–43
    values in, 66
Money values. *See also* Value
    clarification; Values
    adult children and, 220–21
    defined, 66–67
    talking about, 108–11
More than Money, 244
Morgan Memorial Cooperative
    Industries and Stores, 98
Mothers on the Move, Inc., 167
Myers-Briggs Type Indicator, 223

Nanny shadow, 26
New York Society of CPAs, 233
New York Times Magazine, 225
New York University (NYU)
    Family Wealth Institute, xvi,
        221
Newly acquired wealth, 223–28
Newman, Paul, 98
Newman's Own, 98
North Star Fund, 167

Obsessive-compulsive money
management. *See*
Overregulators, in money
management
Ohio State University, 63
Onassis, Jacqueline Kennedy,
196–97
One Percent Club, 244
Open Minds to Equality
(Schniedewind & Davidson),
143, 147
Our Lady of the Wayside, 99
Overprotectiveness, 26, 28
Overregulators
attachment and, 242
in money acquisition (avoidant),
41, 44
in money management
(obsessive-compulsive), 43,
44
in money use (miser), 42, 44

Parkes, Colin Murray, 22
Philanthropic Initiative, Inc., 153,
169, 244
Philanthropy, xviii, 28, 105, 112–13,
153–76, 210, 227–28, 232,
237–38
charity vs., 153
estate planning and, 193, 195–98
getting started, 157–62
as neutral ground for discussion,
176
opportunities for. *See*
Community foundations;
Family foundations; Public
charities
psychological impact of, 155–56
resources, 243–45
roadblocks to, 156–57

taking action, 172–76
token, 114
Philanthropy News Digest, 244
Philanthropy News Network
Online, 244
Pillsbury, Sarah, 167, 237
Pipher, Mary, 238, 239
Postponed Generation, The (Littwin),
xv, 213
Poulter, Stephan, 223
Private foundations. *See* Family
foundations
Public charities, 162, 163–68
social-change foundations, 163,
166–68
traditional, 163–66
Purchasing power, 4

QPRT (Qualified Personal
Residence Trust), 192
Quarterly Journal of Economics, 186
Quest, 151

Raths, Louis, 69
Reality Check, 233
Rebellion-and-rescue dependency,
214
Reflective dialogue, 21–22, 96–97,
239
Reiss, Steven, 63
Religion and philanthropy, 154
Remarriage, 203, 206. *See also*
Adopted children; Divorce;
Stepchildren
Rescuing, 124, 214, 218–19
Rist, Ray, 143
Robin Hood Was Right (Collins &
Rogers), 155
Rockefeller, John D., 42
Rogers, Pam, 155

Rokeach, Milton, 61
Role confusion (developmental
    stage), 31–32, 35, 155
Role models. *See* Money heroes
Rosen, Harvey S., 186

Salvation Army, 163–64, 168, 244
Sameroff, Arnold, 97
Sanger, Carla, 165
Saving, 103–4
Savings accounts, 105–6, 107
Schenkel, Jilliene T., 114, 153–54
Schnaiberg, Allan, 214
Schniedewind, Nancy, 143, 147
School, 29, 149
School curriculum (on diversity),
    142–45
Science fairs, 143
Secure attachment, 17, 18–22, 98
    studies on, 241–43
    in trust stage of development,
        24–25
Secure relationship with money,
    40–41, 44, 45, 50
Self-fulfilling prophecy, 143
Self-regulation, 19
Sentence completion exercise,
    71–73
Shame (developmental stage),
    25–26, 34
Shelter of Each Other, The (Pipher),
    238
Siblings, trouble with, 226
Siegel, Daniel J., 98
Simon, Sidney, 69
Single parents, 24
    adoption by, 203, 207
16 PF, 223
Smith, Hyrum W., 67
So what syndrome, 237

Social capital, 198
Social-change foundations, 163,
    166–68
Societal curriculum (on diversity),
    142–45
Spirituality, 237
Stand and Deliver (film), 144
Stanford University School of
    Medicine, 234
Stein Roe Young Investors Fund,
    228
Stengel, Casey, 232
Stepchildren, 206–9
Stereotypes, 148–49
Stevenson-Hinde, Joan, 22
Stock, gifts of, 228, 229
Strange experiment, 241–42
Stress and newly acquired wealth,
    224, 227
Strong Interest Inventory, 223
StudentMarket.com, 234
Sun, David, 99

Talking about money, 85–116
    as an abstract concept, 95–99
    age differences and, 102–8
    avoiding contradictions between
        deeds and, 112–16
    other subjects related to, 86–89
    with spouse, 56–57
    ten worst things to say, 89–94
    values imparted in, 108–11
Talking piece, 174
Tax-exclusive systems, 179
Tax-inclusive systems, 179
Taxes
    estate, 179–80, 196–97, 198
    gift, 179
Teachable times, 99–101, 172–73
Teardowns, 7

Television, 8–9, 10, 102–3, 104, 233
  diversity training via, 147–48
  reality programming on, 236
  "Television and Socialization of
    Young Children" (study),
    147–48
Tempelsman, Maurice, 196
Therapy, 54–56
Tikkum Olam, 154
Time
  lack of, 8
  as money, 92
  for proper parenting, 238–39
  spent on considering values,
    82–83
Tithing, 154, 158, 196
Toilet training, 26
Traditional charities, 163–66
Trust (developmental stage), 23–25,
    33–34
Trust agreements, 194, 195
Trustees, 180, 194, 195
Trusts, 179, 180–81
  charitable income, 196–97
  example of, 245–48
  four most common mistakes,
    198–201
  incentive-based, 191–93
  as money management tools,
    193–95
  protection provided by, 180, 195
  talking to children about, 184–87
  values communicated through,
    181–83, 200–201, 245–48
Tu, John, 99
Tzedakah, 154

UCLA Center for the Study of
  Evaluation, 166
UCLA Estate Planning Institute, xv

UCLA Medical Center, 165
Underregulators
  attachment and, 242
  in money acquisition (insatiable),
    41–42, 44
  in money management (chaotic),
    43, 44
  in money use (overspender), 42,
    44
University of Kansas Center for
  Research on the Influences of
  Television on Children,
  146–46
University of Miami, 38
University of Michigan, 97
U.S. Trust, 184
Use of money. *See* Money use

Value clarification, 67–82, 85
  acting, 76–82
  choosing among alternatives,
    74–76
  on diversity, 145–46
  identifying what is important,
    70–74
Value hypocrisy, 65
Values, xvii, 34, 59–83, 210, 232. *See
  also* Money values
  defined, 61–66
  emotional, intellectual, and
    behavioral aspects, 65
  estate planning and, 181–83,
    200–201, 245–48
  newly acquired wealth and, 227
Virtual affluence, 3
Virtual foundations, 173–74
Virtue of Prosperity (D'Souza), 144
Visa Buxx, 211
Vocational testing, 222–23
Voigt, Ken, 99

Volunteer Vacations, 150–51
Volunteerism, 157–60, 172, 174–76

WalMart, 185
Walton, S. Robson, 185–86
WCVB-TV, 147
What Matters Most (Smith &
    Blanchard), 67
Wolff, Edward N., 139
Women's Exchange, 98
Woodard, Alfre, 155
Workaholism, 115
Working parents, 24, 205

World Horizons International, 151
"World of Difference Institute"
    program, 147
Worthwhile endeavors, 221–22
Wright, John C., 148

"Yes, You Can" (Department of
    Education), 243
Ylvisaker, Paul, 169
Your Money, Your Self (Matthews),
    86

Zakaat, 154